"At Least You'll Be Married To A Doctor"

Managing Your Intimate Relationship Through Medical School

Jordyn Paradis Hagar

outskirtspress

DENVER, COLORADO

Table of Contents

Part Four: Establishing a New Way

Part Five: Moving Forward

Introduction

"At least you'll be married to a doctor."

If you are in a committed relationship with a medical student, and someone has not already said this to you, just wait, because someone will.

At times people say it flippantly, at times jokingly, and at times jealously. But what do they really mean?

I always think they mean that regardless of your present reality, at least your partner will provide you with financial security in the future. I can never seem to find another interpretation. At best this is accidentally insulting, insinuating that financial gain motivates you. Much worse, it can leave you and any bystanders with some rather uninformed messages about med school.

This statement assumes that the end result of becoming a doctor is worth the means of going through med school. This can come from two different perspectives. Some people assume that becoming a doctor takes less work than it actually does, so they believe that the 'end is worth the means' because the 'means' involved minimal effort. On the other hand, some people know the challenges involved in this process, but they believe that everything that occurs along the way is worth the struggle because it will result in such a desirable end goal.

Both of these conceptualizations have potentially damaging implications if you are trying to manage an intimate relationship while in med school. In reality, the path to becoming a doctor takes a great deal of work, and while the end result may be worth some of the means taken to get there, it is certainly not worth all means. This has even more significance if a med student is in a committed relationship because then any means taken impact not only his own life, but his partner's life as well.

After hearing the above statement uttered by so many well intended but misguided people, I have developed this standard response: "If I wanted to be married to a doctor, I would have married a doctor... not a med student".

Herein lies the purpose of this book.

Medical school is frequently seen not only as an educational experience, but also as a rite of passage, permitting the successful to earn the coveted title of Doctor. If your goal is to be a doctor, you go to medical school. You work ridiculously hard and do everything in your power to not lose this opportunity. You deal with the long hours, the constant studying, the lack of sleep, the fear of not knowing if you know enough, and the absence of pleasure and leisure in your life because this is your dream, and in order to reach your dream, you need to complete medical school.

Some of us do not want to become doctors, though. Some of us do not have to go to medical school to fulfill our dreams, and yet we still find ourselves seriously impacted by this process. We are the significant others of medical students.

It is hard to have a relationship with one member in medical school. At times it feels absolutely impossible. For some couples it takes too much work for it to feel worthwhile. Others find it worth the hard work and find a way to continue to grow, even in spite of and sometimes because of the obstacles on this path.

I chose to write this book because my husband and I were fortunate and found a way to make our relationship work through med school. We know other couples that made it work, but we also know couples that did not. At one point, a friend of mine half jokingly suggested that I write a book on this subject, and that resonated with me. As a therapist, I like to bring useful resources to people in difficult situations, and as the significant other of someone in med school, I liked to talk about being the significant other of someone in med school! I knew I was not the only one who struggled with this role, and so I decided to share my experiences with others in the hopes that it might provide some help along the way.

I did not write this book as an expert or researcher. I present very few concrete facts to you. As I said, I am a therapist, so I may have above average emotional awareness and relational understanding, but that is the biggest claim at 'expertise' I am willing to make in this book. My training and work as a therapist have certainly impacted my perspective and interpretation of what transpires in our relationship, and I am sure that will be evident in my writing. However, I wrote this book primarily as a member of a relationship impacted by medical school.

I wrote this book for the significant others in relationships with medical students because I wish someone had been able to better prepare me. I wrote this book for medical students in relationships because I wish someone had been able to better prepare my husband. I also wrote this book for me. Medical school impacted my life in many ways, and this book helps me to feel a very personal benefit for having lived through this period of time.

This book contains parts of our story. It also contains pieces of the stories of couples we know. From these experiences, I present to you the lessons we have learned, and continue to learn, along the way. Relationships are ever growing, and so this book is not a how-to manual, and it has no magic ending. My goal is to provide some illumination about what to expect. I want to explore the process of how and when the difficult times emerge, and I want to present you with some steps, skills, and perspectives that can help you traverse through these difficult times. We are a couple committed to making it, and we have had to learn many lessons along the way. I present them to you in the hopes that they can benefit you in some way and ease your journey down this difficult, though not impossible, path.

Part One of this book provides an introduction to the process of medical school and medicine as well as a brief introduction to my husband and me. Part Two explores in detail the often unexpected yet extremely powerful relational changes and emotional experiences that can occur when your med student deals with the most overwhelming and demanding parts of med school. Part Three outlines a variety of concepts, perspectives, tools, and strategies that you can use to start moving your relationship away from a stress driven system and toward a healthier balance. Part Four specifically addresses the ultimate shift back to a more equal and sustainable relationship. Part Five looks toward the future by considering the process of residency, making future plans, and addressing some more macro level concerns.

I would like to leave you with a couple of notes. Throughout this book I will generally refer to the med student as 'he' and to the significant other as 'she'. I do this solely because this is how it exists in our relationship and I needed shorthand. The concepts in this book are not restricted to relationships only with this particular gender configuration. Further, I will frequently refer to "your med student" as meaning 'the med student in your relationship'. Again, I needed shorthand and do not mean for you to interpret this in any other way.

Sections of this book primarily address the significant other, some directly address the med student, and other parts address both together. I have done this for emphasis and to help bring awareness to the fact that certain components will have specific use to the significant others or to the med students. However, I strongly encourage both members of the relationship to read the entire book in order to gain the fullest possible understanding of what can transpire for you and your partner both as individuals and together as a unit during this challenging time.

Part One
Setting the Foundation

1
Becoming A Doctor

Before we can discuss how med school impacts our relationships, we first need to understand med school. This chapter outlines the steps involved in med school as well as in the overall process of becoming a doctor.

Applying to med school is a multi-step process. Whether a student decides to enter med school directly from college, after taking some time off, or by changing careers, he must first take the MCAT. This is the standardized test required for applying to med school, comparable in purpose to the SAT for undergraduate admissions or the GRE for graduate admissions. However, the score of this exam weighs more heavily than either the SATs or the GREs do in their respective processes.

After receiving their MCAT score, applicants fill out a primary application online and pay a fee in order to submit their application to the schools they choose. Some applicants only apply to a few programs while others apply to dozens. Once schools receive the primary application, they decide if the applicant merits a secondary application and notify him if he is eligible. Submitting secondary applications requires more paperwork and also comes with a second fee.

Based on the secondary applications, prospective students will be granted an interview, put on a wait list, or rejected without an interview. Depending on where the applicant applied, these interviews could potentially be anywhere in the country. The applicant completes as many interviews as he chooses and then waits to hear through a rolling admissions process if he is accepted, rejected, or wait listed at the places he interviewed. Programs are required to let all applicants know of their status by a specific date, and by this date applicants can no longer hold multiple acceptances. They need to make a decision and commit to one program.

Once applicants have committed to one program, then movement on the waitlists increases. If a school has not filled all of its first year slots, it will move people off their waitlist and offer them acceptance. The prospective student then accepts or rejects this offer. Some applicants will make a commitment to one program but then break this commitment if they get an offer at a more desirable program that has taken them off their waitlist. This then creates further movement within the system, and it is possible that applicants could still receive acceptances up to a couple weeks into the start of the school year.

Some people say the hardest part of med school is getting in. There are extraordinarily high standards to get into a program, and it is certainly a process that requires a great deal of time and money. The waiting and ongoing possibility of some unknown emerging offer can make planning during this time period near impossible. Some people experience uncertainty about their placement up until the last minute. Others may find themselves accepted to their first choice program and have their path determined very early on.

Once a student has made his ultimate commitment, he relocates if he has to, and he starts med school. The first two years of school generally consist of coursework. A med student will study such subjects as anatomy, physiology, histology, genetics, biochemistry, neurobiology, microbiology, pathology, pharmacology, behavioral science, and physical diagnosis, among others. Some programs organize their curriculum to be 'subject based' which means studying each of these subjects one at a time. Other programs use a more 'systems based' curriculum that involves studying different systems in the body and applying each of the subjects listed above as it pertains to a particular body system. Each method has its pros and cons, and people have differing amounts of success with each method depending on their strengths and background.

While it is certainly difficult to get into med school, the reality is that all of med school is hard. Unless a med student is an exceptionally smart and perfectly skilled test taker, it is reasonable to expect a med student to study all the time. I do not say that jokingly, lightly, or flippantly; I truly mean all the time.

Generally, students have four hours or more of lecture a day, and they are expected to know, understand, and remember everything from those lectures as well as from any reading that might be associated with it. A rule of thumb exists that for every hour of lecture attended, students then study that lecture for two more hours that day. If you assume four hours of lecture a day and you do the math, this means that over the course of a 24 hour day, students attend four hours of lecture, study for eight hours, and have twelve hours left over a day for sleeping, eating, taking breaks, and driving to and from school.

OK, you say, that doesn't sound too bad. However, this does not include any extra lectures (consider for every one hour of extra lecture, that is another two hours of study time), any labs (which happen weekly in some courses), any clinical requirements (some schools have first and second year students participate in clinical work and write notes on their patients), and any small group requirements (some schools have required small group work connected with some of their classes). These are not uncommon requirements. My husband, Mike, had all of this at his school, and this quickly turns those twelve leftover hours into far fewer.

This represents the minimum amount of time a student could spend working a day, and most students work much more than the minimum required. Additionally, this total does not include any review and studying done specifically to prepare for an exam. Preparing for exams will not only take up the rest of a med student's free time, it will also often leave him wishing he had even more time to study. If Mike did all of this exactly as described here, he would have slept for about five hours a night.

And there were many times he did.

Now, if you are the significant other of someone in med school, and you read this description, you notice something missing.

Where are you in this list?

We will address that later.

For now, back to the process of medical school.

The first two years of med school involve coursework and resemble the description above. Not everyone suffers equally. People have varying levels of study skills, efficiency, and memory retention. Some med students come to the first years of med school with a strong foundation of study skills, and they feel comfortable in their method of approaching the material and studying. Other students struggle to find a method that works for them. This may involve a constant changing of strategies or an over-reliance on a method that is not necessarily efficient or useful. These students may spend the entire two years struggling to find a way that works; others may ultimately find something that makes them feel comfortable. Significant other, you may find yourself in the role of sounding board, brainstormer, or cheerleader as your med student seeks to find a suitable method of studying. This may take months or even the entire two years. Your experience during these two years will differ based on the strengths of your med student, but even the strongest of students work extremely hard during this time.

After completing these two years, students take the first test in a three part series known as the medical licensing exam. These tests, once all completed, allow a physician to become licensed. After second year, students will take the first part, or step one. This is generally considered the most difficult part, and many students take about one month upon completing second year to study for and take it. This test covers all that a med student has learned over the past two years, and a student's score on this test matters a great deal when it comes time to apply for residency.

After passing step one of the licensing exam, med students complete two years of rotations. During these two years, med students do clinical work. They spend four to twelve weeks shadowing, learning, and gaining experience in different specialties. Third year in most schools includes rotations in family medicine, internal medicine, surgery, pediatrics, obstetrics and gynecology, and psychiatry. Within each of these, students may experience a variety of settings and sub-specialties. For example, within obstetrics and gynecology, a student might spend time doing labor and delivery, gynecological surgery, and outpatient clinic, among other things. Within surgery, a student may be on the service of vascular surgery, cardiothoracic surgery, or plastic surgery, among others.

After completing third year, most students take step two of the licensing exam. Some schools require that students complete this prior to starting fourth year; others only require it prior to graduation. Students tend to study two to four weeks for this exam. Step two contains two components, a clinical part and a written part. The clinical part of the exam is only offered in a select few locations in the country, so many students have to travel to take this part of the exam. The scores on step two seem to matter a bit less than those from step one, though it is still important to pass.

Med students generally have some requirements to complete during their fourth year, but they also have more time to choose electives and further pursue areas of interest. They also have the option of applying for 'away rotations' which are rotations completed at other programs. Med students apply for these about six months before the anticipated start date. Students can access many of these, though not all, through an online application service called the Visiting Student Application Service. There are no interviews. Decisions are based solely on the application, and students are either accepted or not.

Away rotations provide students with extra experiences in a particular specialty, learning opportunities with different doctors and hospital systems, and more knowledge about and exposure to programs they are considering for residency. Away rotations can help students to determine if a program might be a good fit for their extended training in residency. Students also hope that they will have the opportunity while working at a program to show their reliability and reassure the program director that they are sound residency candidates. However, students do run the risk of leaving the rotation having not made the impression they had hoped to make.

Whether a student completes away rotations or not, he will begin planning for residency during the summer before his fourth year. Residency comes after completion of fourth year, and it is the extended training required before becoming a board certified physician. Students will have exposure to many specialties during their time spent on rotations, and they will choose one to pursue more thoroughly through residency. Depending on the specialty, residencies can last between three to six years.

During fourth year, students engage in the residency match process. They will first apply to programs in the fall of their fourth year. Then from October through January, programs will offer interviews to students they wish to consider for their residency positions. Students will travel to these programs and partake in interviews. After all interviews have been completed around mid February, students create a list of the programs where they interviewed and rank them according to their preferences. Programs also create a ranked list of the students they have interviewed. These lists are all submitted to a centralized computer system that works to match students and programs in such a way that the most participants are granted the highest preference possible. Essentially, the system seeks to make the most people as happy as they can be. One Monday in March, students find out whether they matched into a program or not, and then the following Thursday is known as Match Day. On this day nationwide, med students find out which residency program they will attend. The student's assigned program is binding.

A small portion of med students will go through the match process and not actually match with a program. Similarly, some programs may not fill all of their available positions through the match. Currently, if a student does not match, he will be notified the Monday before Match Day, and he then has the opportunity to participate in what is known as the Scramble. There is a plan to change this process for the 2012 match, but at this point, the Scramble still exists as described here.

At the same time that students learn that they have not matched, a list is released of all the remaining available positions. Unmatched students consult this list and start contacting these programs in order to find a program that will take them into their unmatched position. Some people in this situation will find a program to join; however, they may need to settle for a program in a specialty other than the one they originally pursued.

Regardless of how or whether they match, students graduate with their MD during the spring of their fourth year, and by late June or early July, most start their residency programs.

The first year of residency is known as "intern year" and it is traditionally the most difficult, time consuming, and grueling. Generally, at the end of intern year, residents take step three of the medical licensing exam. This portion involves two days of testing, again with a written and clinical component. Over the next several years of the program, residents take on more responsibility and continue developing their skills. At the end of residency, residents take the board exam in their specific area of practice. Upon completion of their program and passing their board exam, they become board certified physicians who can now pursue jobs in a more traditional manner.

The option does still remain of pursuing a fellowship. A fellowship involves even more training in a sub-specialty branching from the practice area of residency. For example, someone who chose internal medicine for his residency can then pursue a fellowship in one of several areas, including cardiology, pulmonology, oncology, or endocrinology, among others. A fellowship is not required to practice medicine, and many people do not further sub-specialize.

Applying for fellowships generally involves another matching process, though some fellowships are applied for like jobs without the matching component. In general, there are fewer fellowship positions, and only certain programs across the country offer fellowships. If a student knows he would like to pursue a fellowship after residency, he may also try to match into a residency program that has a fellowship program in the same institution.

This brief overview of the process of medical training is by no means a comprehensive guide, and it emphasizes the logistics of medical school. Further, every medical student does not complete this sequence in an uninterrupted course. Some students do not pass exams, courses, or years of med school. Depending on a program's policies, students may have the chance to make up single exams if they do not pass, or they may need to repeat entire courses. If students do not pass multiple courses or barely pass throughout the year, they may need to repeat a year. Some students take a year off during med school, or they may choose to do a year of research between second and third year. They may have to repeat a rotation or more than one rotation. They may have to start residency late or apply for residency with the next class. Some people choose to take a year off before residency. Some people have life emergencies that disrupt the course of med school. There are so many different ways to complete this path, and each journey does not necessarily look the same. I simply present here the basics as a way of creating a foundation and a starting point for our journey through med school.

2
Our Relationship

I know you are not reading this book because you are interested in the specifics of my relationship with my husband. Since I plan to incorporate the lessons we have learned throughout this book, though, I think it is important that you have at least a general context for our circumstances.

Mike and I are originally from New England. We met through friends of ours in August of 2005. I was finishing my masters degree in social work, and he was working and applying to medical school. When we started dating, it was with the understanding that in about a year, Mike would move wherever he would attend med school.

I was going to graduate with my masters degree just before Mike would start med school. We knew from the beginning of our relationship that if, by the time I graduated, we could see a future together and med school did require relocating,

I would move with him in order to continue our relationship. We agreed that once med school ended, we would do everything we could to return to New England, and that plan actually never changed.

We continued in a relationship for just under a year before we relocated for med school. During that year, Mike did what he could to prepare me for what was to come. He had some experience taking med school level classes, and so he could describe the time commitment and energy that it would involve. I knew we would encounter difficult circumstances, particularly during the first two years while he had to study a great deal. I also knew we would likely need to leave New England and our entire support system. We did the best we could to prepare, though we also knew that we could never fully prepare for all the changes that were coming.

The med school Mike decided to attend brought us from New England to the Mid Atlantic region in July of 2006. We left family and friends and moved to a place where we knew no one. We did not just start med school; we started an entire new chapter in our lives. This certainly impacted our experience during this time since we not only had to learn to navigate the stress and demands of med school, we simultaneously had to establish a life for ourselves. This meant learning to live and work together as a couple, handling each other's stresses, cultivating new friendships and support systems, starting new employment, and learning a new location, all while also dealing with med school.

As I said, I am employed as a therapist, and I am trained as a social worker. I had already completed all of my schooling by the time Mike started med school, and I worked full time while Mike attended school. Throughout med school only Mike and I lived together. We became engaged just before the end of his first year, and we married at the end of his second. We did not have any children during this time.

Mike and I had a strong relationship going into med school, and it became much stronger over time. At times this was challenged and our relationship required more attention and work. We both individually and together as a couple faced some very difficult periods, but we continued to grow together and remained committed to our relationship and our long-term lives together.

Prior to starting med school, we had a general idea of what to expect regarding the time that med school would require from Mike, but we were not ultimately prepared for just how strenuous and consuming it became at times. We also did not have any conception of just how taxing this commitment to med school would be on our emotional lives and in our relationship with one another.

Early on, before we knew how emotionally demanding med school could become, we focused our emotional energy more on leaving our families and relocating to another part of the country. Over time, though, Mike's emotional energy became wrapped up in the demands of med school, while mine became focused on the losses, the loneliness, and the impact med school had on our relationship.

I want to acknowledge here, for all significant others, that you will likely have moments when you wish that your med student wanted to be anything but a doctor. I certainly had moments I wished that. I would daydream at times about Mike quitting school and us starting over doing something entirely new. I still have moments when I think that almost anything would be easier than having a partner involved in medicine.

At some point in time, you will also likely question whether your relationship is worth all the effort that med school demands from you. In the end, only you can answer that question, but you need to know that you may feel like this sometimes, and that is okay. These feelings are normal, and the fact that Mike and I had to learn this on our own is part of the reason I have written this book.

While I definitely had times I wished Mike was not interested in medicine, I also loved how passionate and driven Mike would become with regard to medicine. As we moved past the most difficult times of med school, it became very rewarding to see him excited about what he does on a daily basis.

In the end, we go through the difficulties of med school because we want our partner to be happy in his career. Med school affects both partners, though, and until now, no real resources have existed to help prepare us for the more emotional aspects of what can transpire in a med school impacted relationship. Many of the ideas presented in this book develop from the impact that med school can have on your emotional and relational experiences, and so we will start there now.

Part Two
Adapting

3

Emotional Realities

When your med student first starts med school and begins adjusting to its requirements, your relationship will start on a journey that involves adapting and adjusting of its own as well. The beginning of med school generally creates a great deal of logistical and emotional change for both med students and significant others due to the new time commitments and requirements it presents. Every relationship is unique and has its own strengths and challenges, so the emotional and relational impact of med school will not be the same in every relationship. However, the themes presented in this chapter and in the next two are very common within med school impacted relationships, particularly as both partners adjust to the med school process.

Times of Overwhelm

I introduce here the concept of 'overwhelm'. In writing this book, I have tried to find a word that adequately explains what can occur at times during med school. Ultimately, the only sufficient word I have found is 'overwhelm'. There is something powerful in using 'overwhelm' as a noun. I find that it immediately suggests how a set of logistical circumstances and emotional experiences can so completely and utterly rule a period of time. 'Being overwhelmed' resonates as an emotional experience. 'It was overwhelming' seems to primarily address circumstances. I wanted a word that combines both the emotional and circumstantial because that is the sentiment that I need to convey.

As a concept, overwhelm is certainly not restricted to experiences in med school. It has increasingly been used in time management discourse, and I am sure people who experience intense illnesses, confront life altering losses, or encounter any kind of consuming circumstances in their lives can relate to this idea. Throughout this book, though, I will use the concept of overwhelm to describe what can occur at times during med school, first as it relates to an individual med student, and then as it relates to your relationship as a whole.

As you go through the process of med school, you and your partner will likely experience a time of true overwhelm. For some couples, this will occur primarily as the med student adjusts to the new requirements of med school, and then it will subside. Some couples may experience a relatively seamless transition into med school and then feel more stress as the coursework intensifies into the second year. Some may encounter more overwhelm with coursework, while others may with clinical work. Some may only experience difficult periods when preparing to take the licensing exams. Some couples may not experience these difficulties at all, and some may experience them near constantly for the entirety of med school.

There are no real universal patterns regarding the specific timing of overwhelm. A couple's experience of this overwhelm differs based on the couple's strengths, the med student's strengths, and the dynamics of the particular med school program. It is also impacted by the point at which the relationship begins, whether before or during med school, as well as the particular moment in time during med school. If a couple goes through the entire four years of med school together, they will likely experience more intense overwhelm during the first two years and then see it subside over the last two, but again this is not universal.

The timing of overwhelm is not the same for every couple, but the process can look very similar. Because of this, I will focus more on the stages in our relationships as opposed to the stages in med school as we continue to discuss the impact of overwhelm.

Going into our med school experience, I assumed that even with the challenging logistical realities that med school creates, our emotional reality would remain fairly constant. We very quickly began to see, though, that both the logistical and emotional realities we had prepared for were unrealistic. We had prepared for Mike to be busy and spend much of his time studying, but in reality he spent all of his time studying. It was much more challenging to stay on track than we had originally anticipated. This generally meant no free time together, different bed times, and little to no time for anything else.

Med students get tired. They will often work for fifteen to eighteen hours a day with only short and infrequent breaks, every day for several months. This kind of tired is about more than just sleepiness; it involves crankiness, irritability, and a preoccupation with not having done enough. Many med students feel like they do not have enough time to do what is required and that they always have more to do. This can lead to the feeling that any break is a waste of time.

Med students may find it hard to engage in activities that actually assist in self care, like exercising, going out, working on hobbies, or taking breaks, because they may feel as if they do not have enough time to do those things. Significant other, you may notice your med student talking about what he studies, even when taking a break, because it may feel impossible for him to think about anything other than medicine and what he has been learning.

Med students usually get overwhelmed at various points along the way. Many med students will feel fear or worry about getting behind, not passing exams, or not knowing enough material. When they experience these feelings, it becomes very difficult for them to find the merit in thinking about or doing something unrelated to medicine.

Med students will likely have moments of depression. Many med students have times when they ask themselves if all of the effort is worth the ultimate goal. They will experience sadness and loss at not being able to attend events, engage with people, and pursue other areas of interest and leisure.

Med students will experience this kind of overwhelm at times, and they will still need to continue to work at their intense pace.

Significant other, when your med student struggles with a period of overwhelm, you will likely find that he has little to no time or brain space left to spend on you. It is normal to find yourself feeling lonely, unsupported, unappreciated, disconnected, or distant at these times. It can be extremely hard to come home from your day and encounter someone who has absolutely no capacity to be interested in or supportive of what has transpired in your day. It can feel much lonelier to sit next to a person who cannot engage with you in a meaningful way than it would to sit in a room by yourself.

Does this mean your med student does not love you? Absolutely not. It means he is so overwhelmed with this stage in med school and he needs time to adjust to it. Will it always be like this? No, it will not. This period of overwhelm can last for a long time, and for most couples it does involve some active work to manage, but it changes over time.

Med school has started, and eventually a period of overwhelm descends. The med student becomes singly focused on med school in order to stay afloat, and the significant other essentially finds herself without the benefit of her partner. Where does this leave us? It leaves us aware that our relationship no longer seems quite as typical as one not impacted by med school. It also leaves us wondering what to do about this.

We will first explore how a med school relationship is structurally different from a relationship unaffected by med school. Then we will look at how these times of overwhelm impact the dynamics within our relationships.

Conceptualizing a Med School Relationship

In a typical intimate relationship that does not involve children, there are two people, or entities, and ideally they function with an amount of equality between them. Neither has more or less of a say than the other. Neither demands more or less of the other than they themselves would be willing to give in return.

When one member of the relationship is in med school, though, there are actually three entities present in the relationship: the med student, the significant other, and med school. Every entity in the relationship has needs, and every entity makes demands on the others. The med student has to answer both to the significant other and to med school, just as the significant other answers both to med school and to the med student. Sometimes the med student is the priority, sometimes the significant other is, and sometimes med school is.

In this kind of relationship, we consider med school in our lives and in our plans the way we would consider another person. We split our effort, attention, and resources not just between one another, but with med school as well. This kind of relationship does not split 50-50 (%) the way a more typical relationship does. At least during the times of overwhelm, it is, at best, 33-33-33 (%).

At times this third entity can feel like a child. You will find yourselves putting your own needs aside in order to meet the needs of med school. In those moments, nothing else matters. Your med student will find himself devoting all his energy to med school. Significant other, you will likely find yourself devoting at least some of your energy to making your med student's life easier. There will be many times, especially during times of overwhelm, when you both sacrifice meeting at least some of your needs in order to better meet the needs of med school.

This third entity can also feel like a mistress. At times your med student will be excited by, impassioned by, and ready to sacrifice anything for med school. He will come home after working long hours, more excited about what has transpired at the hospital than about finally being home. Significant other, you may find him ready to give up sleep, leisure time, and relaxation all for med school, but not for you. Your med student has very little choice about the hours he works and the sacrifices he makes for med school, but you will likely see him continue to give it his time not only because he has to, but also because he loves it and because he wants this. He has a passion for this, and so his sacrifices lead to a reward. Significant other, your sacrifices in this process do not generally lead to the same tangible gratification, at least not initially.

Whether this entity at times feels like a child, a mistress, or just a consuming, demanding abyss, it is a third entity in our relationships, and it shares in our relationship resources. At first, neither partner will get 50% of the relationship resources because at least a portion will go to med school.

Because of this, different kinds of complications can occur. The most common, and disruptive, happens when we, as significant others, forget that med school and our med student are not the same entity. This is so common and so potentially damaging that much of the next three chapters focuses on this theme.

Less destructive, but still frustrating, is how others may judge your relationship. If a typical healthy relationship operates with the 50-50 code, and your relationship, unbeknownst to an outsider, involves splitting resources three ways, that outsider will frequently assume that your relationship is unhealthy or unbalanced in some way. That person simply does not know that you have to split the resources in your relationship three ways instead of just two.

I mention this three-entity conceptualization here for several reasons. It can be useful when trying to understand your own relationship and when trying to conceptualize your relationship to outsiders who do not understand the demands of the situation. Additionally, it will now serve as the foundation for our discussion of the dynamics of a med school relationship.

Emotion Work

"Emotion work" is a sociological term that started to receive more intent focus in the 1970s and 1980s with the work of Arlie Russel Hochschild. It is loosely comprised of two components: "emotion management" and "feeling rules" (Hochschild, 2001).

Emotion management refers to the fact that people can choose how they respond when they experience a particular feeling. We have many options available to us when we need to manage feelings. We have the option of expressing our feelings through conversations or arguments. We can try to release our feelings through physical activity or creative expression like music or art. We can also keep our feelings inside and either dwell on them or try not to think about them. Sometimes we avoid thinking about our feelings by distracting ourselves, turning our attention to something else, or engaging in another activity.

Emotion work also involves the concept of feeling rules. Feeling rules are the socially accepted and expected ways of experiencing and handling feelings. People expect other people to cry when they are sad, yell when they are angry, and laugh when they are happy. People are less accepting when other people laugh during sad or intense moments or act down when life is going well.

Society suggests certain limits on the expression of feelings; yelling when angry is more permissible than hitting or hurting someone, just as crying when sad is more acceptable than hurting oneself. People also expect that an emotional reaction be in proportion to the situation that has occurred. For example, yelling may make sense if one spouse cheats on the other but not if he forgets to do the dishes.

In addition, feeling rules cover how we expect others to respond to us when we experience and express a feeling. If we express sadness in an appropriate manner, we expect to receive support, sympathy, and attention. If we feel anxious and express this in an acceptable way, we expect for someone to help console or counsel us. On the contrary, if our emotional expression is out of proportion to the situation, then it makes sense that we would not receive a supportive or patient response. If I scream hysterically because I have to clean up a mess in the kitchen, my partner is not going to respond sympathetically because I am overreacting. However, if I sigh in frustration and kindly ask my partner for help because I am overwhelmed, I can expect a more positive response.

Emotion work focuses on the idea that people engage in emotion management by taking into account feeling rules. In other words, we try to experience and handle our feelings in a way that the people around us expect and accept, and we try to respond to others' feelings in a way that makes sense given the circumstances and their emotional expression.

These concepts permeate everyone's life to some extent. I introduce them here in our conversation about med school relationships because med school impacts emotion work. I maintain that med school changes emotion work in two primary ways. First, it redefines the feeling rules. Second, it places the responsibility for the emotion work much more heavily on one person.

Redefining Feeling Rules

Every couple is different, and each develops habits, routines, and methods of interacting and communicating that are unique to that partnership. These comprise a couple's feeling rules, and they will differ for each couple to some extent. However, many couples do operate with some of the same basic tenets, such as agreement in the division of labor, expectation to be heard and supported, and anticipation of respect and partnership. These feeling rules tend to generalize to the majority of healthy couples.

I thought that during med school our feeling rules would remain the same as they are for other couples, as described above. We would both have time to talk to one another, express feelings to the other, and be supported and cared for. I assumed that when I experienced a feeling and approached it in accordance with fairly typical feeling rules, then I would get the expected response in my relationship.

Significant others can generally respond to their med students within the context of typical feeling rules. When your med student is anxious or depressed or when he has a need that requires attention, the significant other can generally attend to this in a supportive way.

As we explored earlier, though, during times of med school overwhelm, a med student generally has little, and at times nothing, left to return to the relationship. During times of overwhelm, very little time, attention, and energy get directed toward the significant other. Thus, during these times, a significant other cannot always expect the response, support, and care from her partner that typical feeling rules dictate.

Human beings, when repeatedly met with an unappealing response, generally start trying to avoid that response. Significant others, when you are supportive of and engaging toward your partner but receive a lack of support and engagement in return, you will find yourselves wanting to avoid that response. In a typical relationship, you would likely find this inequality unacceptable and put an end to the situation.

However, in your med school relationship, this is expected during times of overwhelm, and you will need to adapt to the temporary circumstances if you want your relationship to last. Within our emotion work analysis, when you consistently encounter broken feeling rules ("I give but do not receive"; "I express myself appropriately and yet do not get the support I expect"), and you also want to sustain your relationship through this difficult time, you will find yourself looking for new feeling rules.

In our home, I rather quickly learned that Mike was too overwhelmed to handle much more than what med school required of him. I found myself doing what I could to manage the household and also to help him in other ways as well. Unbeknownst to me at the time, I was taking in all the messages I was receiving in our new circumstances, exploring our broken feeling rules, and floundering for a new way to be. As I acted in new ways and Mike responded to those actions, we accidentally started the process of creating our household's new feeling rules. Taking into account all the logistics of med school, it is not surprising that our new feeling rules did not, for a while, resemble those in other households.

One-Sided Emotion Work

Essentially, our new feeling rules largely involved me emotionally supporting both of us for a period of time. I am calling this concept, where one partner takes over the role of nurturing and sustaining the emotional integrity of the relationship for both partners, one-sided emotion work. For now we will discuss creating these new, temporarily adaptive feeling rules, and in later chapters we will explore how to move past the one-sided emotion work into a more permanently healthy set of feeling rules.

What does one-sided emotion work look like? Essentially, it means that one member of the relationship is primarily the giver and the other is primarily the receiver. Significant other, you will primarily be the giver. Does this mean you always have to give? No. Does this mean you will never get to receive? Not at all. Does this mean your med student has the right to take advantage of you and your support? Of course not. It means that more frequently you will find yourself actively supporting your partner and his emotional experience than he will be actively supporting you and your emotional experience. It means that when you have nothing left to give your partner, that will be fine, but he may not have anything to give back to you in that moment either.

It means that for the time being, while your med student struggles with a difficult part of the program and he needs to give medical school all of his resources, you will ensure that your relationship stays functional and healthy and initiate any relationship maintenance work that needs to occur. In the end, you will not only serve as your med student's primary means of emotional support, you will also serve as your own.

This felt like I ran our relationship for a little while. That did not mean that Mike did not want to be in our relationship, that he did not love me, or that he did not appreciate what I did for him, because he did on all counts. It meant that he did not have the brain space or the energy to be as active a participant as he would have liked.

This is not atypical in relationships during times of med school overwhelm, and many couples have talked about the ways that the significant other performs this more one-sided emotion work. It is a survival mechanism to get through this difficult period, and it can be healthy as long as both partners commit to undoing this temporary mechanism once you have moved through the difficult times.

Many significant others have noted the same areas of contention during this part of the med school relationship process. Your med student may take breaks from studying but not stop thinking or talking about medicine. If he does manage to stop thinking about medicine, he may still not attend to anything else. He may tolerate speaking himself, but not listen to what you would like to say. This can come across as impatient, arrogant, or condescending, when in reality, it may be your med student's way of seeking support for his stress and overwhelm. Significant others can find this a lonely and frustrating time because you may actually see and be near your partner but still not connect with him emotionally, physically, or mentally.

Your med student's lack of mental and emotional availability can also lead to you feeling as though you have to think about, consider, plan, and organize all the details that go into managing your daily life and relationship all on your own. It can become frustrating to make these decisions and manage this information alone when it all involves and impacts your partner as well. It can also become frustrating if your med student does manage to attend to what you say only to have him later forget the information when he becomes reabsorbed in his studies.

He may forget what you say! you

In addition, you may experience an issue with regard to having a bad day. Most significant others of med students can tell a story about having had a bad day of some kind, and their med student's response either explicitly or inferentially suggested that their bad day could not begin to compare to the constant 'bad day' of a med student. I can understand how this would either directly or indirectly get communicated. Many med students are truly so overworked, and they do have to continue to work at this pace every single day.

However, that does not take away from the fact that the significant other lives a life, encounters stresses, has bad days, gets tired, and does not feel well. Does this compare to the distress of med school? Sometimes yes, sometimes no. Remember, though, that the significant other often does not have the emotional support from her partner the way that the med student does as a means of dealing with the distress.

This can be a contentious period in the relationship. If you see the feeling rules in your relationship starting to change, though, it makes sense to talk about it with your partner. Make an agreement to temporarily change your feeling rules and engage in more one-sided emotion work, and agree that this change will not be permanent. This kind of emotion work may not feel intuitive, but as explained at the start of this chapter, there really are three entities in your relationship, and you both have to make adjustments because of med school, especially at first.

You do not need to use these feelings rules at all times either. There were moments, like on holiday breaks, when Mike and I would return to our previous feeling rules and engage in more two-sided emotion work. We would talk about all that had happened in the previous semester and what we wanted to work on for the next semester. During those times, we worked on our relationship equally. These conversations and decisions might not have occurred in the way I would have liked during the semester, but I could trust that once a break came, our relationship was healthy enough to restore two-sided emotion work and address what was necessary. In those moments, Mike could do his own emotion work again, and I sought reassurance that some day med school would change and Mike would become a more consistently equal emotional partner in our relationship again.

Conclusion

With new feeling rules and one-sided emotion work, situations do not unfold the way they might in a more typical relationship. You may find your relationship struggling or progressing more slowly in areas where other couples seem to more quickly thrive. It may take longer for you and your partner to develop certain standard arrangements and methods of interacting than it does for other couples. The growing process may take longer and unfold more slowly at times.

Some of these situations will feel unfair. If you were following traditional feeling rules, they would be unfair. We have temporarily changed our feeling rules, though. We have created them and agreed to abide by them of our own free will. That does not change the fact that we do not always like them and at times will yearn for more traditional feeling rules. Fortunately, this framework is not permanent, and from this point forward we will look at how to work toward a more permanently healthy state.

The first step in moving to an ultimate shift in your relationship is to recognize and deal with all of the new feelings that can emerge. Confusion, depression, sadness, loneliness, hopelessness and anger are all common for both partners to experience, and both partners will experience these feelings because of the impact that med school has on your lives. The tools and concepts in this book can help both partners to manage all of the new feelings.

Deal with all that you are feeling!

However, two primary differences exist between the emotional experiences of a med student and those of a significant other. First, as we have described here, med students often have the support of their partners while managing their new feelings, whereas significant others may find themselves dealing with their own new feelings more independently.

Second, med students' feelings generally occur within the context of working toward a goal of their own choosing. They decided to pursue the path to become a doctor, and they can always weigh the obstacles and struggles that produce intense feelings against their end goal. Significant others experience their feelings in a more complex set of circumstances. They did not choose medicine, but their lives are still intricately connected to the process of medicine. Significant others chose the relationship, not the circumstances that exist around it, and so at times it becomes difficult to distinguish between med student and med school.

Because of the complexity of the significant others' emotional experiences, the next two chapters focus more specifically on the significant other and two feelings that have the potential to be damaging personally and relationally if left unattended. In these next two chapters I will use myself as a case example in order to more effectively demonstrate the process of addressing and dealing with these feelings.

* Deal with your feelings!

4

Grieving

The first feeling I want to explore in more detail is grief. Many people think of grief as a reaction to death, but this is not the complete truth. Grief is an emotion associated with loss. Death is a form of loss, but it is not the only form of loss.

Loss can be characterized by any significant change to one's life. A person can experience the loss of a person, a relationship, a job, or a home. A person can experience loss through a move, a natural disaster, a trauma, a divorce, or a marriage. When a baby is born, when a friend moves away, or when your reality changes in some way, a sense of loss can occur. A person can even experience loss when something he expected to happen in the future is no longer going to happen. A change in a person's life is rarely ever all good or all bad. Generally both positive and negative elements exist; while change often leads to some kind of gain or addition, a loss or absence occurs equally as often.

When someone has a loss, he may then experience grief. Elisabeth Kübler-Ross was a psychiatrist who did a great deal of work with death and dying. She developed what is now a commonly recognized model of the five stages of grief. The stages include denial, anger, bargaining, depression, and acceptance (Kübler-Ross, 1969).

Denial is characterized by a psychological inability to acknowledge the reality of the situation. It is accompanied by sentiments such as, "Things are fine" or "This isn't really happening".

When a person experiences anger, he often seeks to find someone to blame for the situation and, as stated, feels anger: "Who is to blame?", "How can this be happening to me?", "This isn't fair!".

Bargaining involves trying to negotiate some kind of exchange for the situation to improve, often times to some kind of higher power: "I will give (something) if...", "I will do anything to make this different".

With depression, a person can experience intense sadness, numbness, hopelessness, or disconnection. People most frequently associate this stage with grief as it generally involves sadness and crying. A person in this stage may question whether he can or should go on: "What's the point? I'm just so sad/low/down/disconnected".

The last stage, acceptance, happens when a person has come to terms with the loss, reaches a point of peace, and is able to start moving forward and engage in future oriented thinking again: "Things will be ok again", "This was a big change in my life, but it does not mean my life is over".

These stages do not occur in a rigidly sequential manner, and people can shift between stages multiple times. Generally, though, people tend to not return to a state of denial once they have acknowledged and accepted the reality of the situation.

I share this with you, because every significant other of a med student that I know has grieved at least one loss that med school has created. Some of our losses are unique to our own circumstances. For example, I moved 500 miles from my friends and family for my husband to go to med school, and I had to grieve that loss. I have a friend whose husband decided on medicine as a second career. She had to grieve the loss of their previous life when they both worked, had more income, and had more free time and freedom together.

Some of our losses are not unique, though. Universally, significant others of med students tend to grieve, to some extent or another, for the life that we had thought we would have before med school entered our lives. This does not mean that we all lost the same vision of life; we just all lost the vision of a life without medicine.

Some med students may go through a similar grieving process, though the details may differ. A med student planned for med school to be a part of his life, where a significant other did not until she entered into the relationship. Even still, a med student may find that med school impacts aspects of his life in ways he had not anticipated. This can trigger a grief reaction of his own since med school has introduced more losses or more intense losses than he had expected.

Case Example

I am going to use myself as a case example in order to help illustrate how grief and the grieving process can impact your emotional reality and the well being of your relationship.

When I used to think about my twenties, I envisioned completing my education and starting my life with someone. I pictured that person and I traveling, exploring, and visiting with family and friends. I counted on free time to enjoy everything we would want to do together.

When we first started med school, I used to think that we could make my vision work, unaffected by med school. Aside from the fact that we lived far away from family, I thought we could achieve most of my vision without too much interruption.

I was in denial, and that changed quickly.

As med school started, it became apparent that Mike did not have free time to share in these leisure activities with me. He did not have nights or weekends off; he had to study all the time. When he had a rare break and did not have to study, he was simply too tired to consider any kind of exertion or excursion. Further, he never had his schedule more than a few months in advance, so it made planning ahead and scheduling trips even more difficult.

Denial passed, and then I experienced anger. I believed for a while that med school ruined my twenties, and I was mad. On a good day I blamed med school. On a bad day I blamed Mike. I was resentful and really could not see the fairness in any of this. I knew that I had made the choice to be with Mike and move to a new area, but as I described in the previous chapter, I had not anticipated the emotional reality of what came next. It became easy to place the blame anywhere else. For now, suffice it to say that this was not a healthy stage for me or for us, but it was a significant stage, and I will discuss it more in the next chapter.

After anger, I entered the stage of bargaining. I had a harder time identifying this stage in my experiences than I did the others, but I ultimately realized that this stage came to me in the form of daydreaming. I never actually pled my case to a higher power or uttered the actual words "I will give anything if...", but I went through a period of time where I daydreamed about every other possible path my life could have taken. I think that my daydreams were my own internal bargain. Without saying the actual words, I was internally negotiating, "If I can just go back, I'll do it differently." In my daydreams I blessed myself with the gift of premonition and figured that somehow, if I could live it all over again, I would know to change my decisions.

In reality, we have no way of knowing the outcome of our decisions without first living through it, so I had no reason to think that I would make any decision differently if I lived my life again. Eventually I realized that, and I got depressed. I had no alternate reality. I had made my choices. I did love Mike, and I did want to spend my life with him. Yet everything I had wanted in my twenties still would not happen the way that I had wanted it to. I cried a lot. I had reached the depression stage in my grief.

It seems a far leap from frequently crying to acceptance. And it is. I am not sure that everyone makes it. I think that is part of the reason so many couples in medicine separate. Acceptance is hard. Many different components have to come together in order to reach acceptance. I had some help from our circumstances.

As most med students do, Mike at times questioned his capabilities as they related to his work load. During these times, he experienced even more stress and anxiety, and I found myself wondering about the possibilities of him repeating portions of the curriculum or having to leave med school. I became unnecessarily fearful of the possibility of Mike not being able to complete med school. Becoming a doctor was Mike's dream, and I could not imagine what would happen if he no longer had that opportunity available to him.

That fear helped me to ultimately find acceptance. Perhaps it was actually for the best that I did not know that having to leave med school was never a realistic option. By believing that this could happen, I began to see that enduring med school was absolutely not the worst option for us. When I compared Mike not becoming a doctor to enduring med school, I saw no comparison. I would without a doubt do whatever was necessary if it meant Mike could follow his dream. And I meant it.

And in meaning it, I started to see things differently.

My twenties were not ruined. They were changed.

And when change happens, there is both good and bad.

Could we hang out with family and friends on a predictable schedule? No.

Could we explore and take trips whenever we wanted? No.

Could we vacation and travel without effort? No.

But we could still see family and friends. We could still explore and take trips. We could still vacation and travel. We had to do these in a different manner than I had anticipated, but we could still do them. In falling in love with Mike when Mike was already in love with medicine, I had to change certain visions I had for my life. But I gained Mike. The rest we would creatively figure out.

And largely we did. We tried to look for opportunities in our circumstances. We strategically organized vacations around friend and family weddings and thus were able to travel places we might not normally have sought out. We took trips to and explored several different nearby cities and attractions. We had friends who were restricted by the same schedule as Mike, so it increased our ability to coordinate and spend time with them. Sometimes, I really wanted to do certain things, and Mike did not have the time to do them with me. That became okay. He and I prioritized the things we really wanted to do together, and I did the other things with other people.

Additionally, so much of our life ended up being positively impacted by what could have easily been interpreted as a negative situation. It took time to reflect and notice all of the good that came out of this difficult period of time, but when we truly looked at the bigger picture, it became easier to find acceptance.

I came to accept that I made my choices. I maybe did not do it with all the information that I have now, but even once I had this information, I chose to stay with Mike. I did not choose med school, but Mike did, and I chose Mike. When I thought that Mike might lose medicine, I could not bear the thought. That is as much my reality as anything else.

I occupy a state of acceptance much of the time now. It has been a journey, though, and I still fluctuate at times. The fluctuations have decreased over time, but certain situations will trigger the other stages again. Fortunately, these other stages occur less intensely and produce less uncertainty than they used to because they have been largely resolved.

I tell you all of this so that you can start to interpret what is happening when your emotions just do not seem to make sense to you anymore. I am also telling you so that you know it is not only okay, but natural, to go through all this. GRIEVE. Something in your life will be different than you expected because of med school. Mourn it. Be angry, be sad, and let yourself feel it. This is grief, it is a process, and it is healthy. Eventually you can reach acceptance, but you cannot do it by pretending everything is fine. You have to acknowledge and experience just how miserable it can be so that when you reach your acceptance, it is of reality. This is a big part of what will ultimately enable you to move to a more stable place personally and in your relationship.

This is Key!

5

Managing Resentment

The second feeling I would like to discuss more thoroughly is resentment. As I alluded to in the previous chapter, the presence of anger seems particularly salient and common among significant others, and this connects very closely with resentment.

The dictionary defines resentment as "Indignation or ill will felt as a result of a real or imagined grievance". As the significant other of a med student, you will experience a variety of grievances. At times you will have focused and immediate grievances such as not being able to go out with your partner on Friday night or having to repeatedly complete one of his chores because he has too much work to do. Other times you will experience grievances for bigger picture disturbances like altering an image you had of your life or creating an imbalance in your relationship for a time. Sometimes a small, immediate grievance will remind you of a longer-term grievance and trigger a dose of resentment that is out of proportion to the immediate situation.

In reality, you can almost always find a grievance when your partner is a med student. Even if no immediate grievance calls your attention, you can probably think real hard about how your life has changed and summon up something to resent. As I am sure you can guess, this potential for very available resentment can cause some problems.

Managing Resentment Through Defense Mechanisms

Defense mechanisms are psychological strategies that help an individual's mind manage stress, anxiety, and unpleasant emotions (Goldstein, 1984; Vaillant, 1992). Many different defense mechanisms exist, and I mention them here because, upon reflection, I have realized that defense mechanisms and managing resentment are closely connected. As stated in the definition, defense mechanisms help to manage unpleasant emotions, and resentment certainly counts as one of those.

We implement defense mechanisms in different ways. Some occur subconsciously and without our awareness while others we can use more purposefully, like coping skills, as our awareness grows. We generally use different strategies at different stages throughout our lives, and a strategy only becomes problematic if it leads to maladaptive patterns in our behavior, such as avoiding difficult events, not acknowledging feelings, or taking feelings out on someone else.

As I reflected on the role that resentment played in my life during the times of med school overwhelm, I was surprised to see how many different defense mechanisms I ended up using. Resentment is a powerful feeling and it took work to manage it. I would like to illustrate for you my journey with resentment and how the defense mechanisms I used to handle it developed and became healthier over time. I hope that this then provides you with a context through which to interpret and understand some of your own experiences with resentment.

Case Example

Let us start with the object of your resentment. Do you resent your significant other, med school in general, or specific practices in med school that make life exceptionally difficult? At different moments you will likely resent each of these, and at moments they will all probably deserve your resentment.

However, we do not always experience resentment in such a clear or logical way. It is difficult to resent an institution. Because of this, grievances regarding med school will often trigger feelings of resentment toward your partner. This is a defense mechanism called displacement, and many of us use this at some point in time. Instead of experiencing your resentment toward the truly objectionable item, in this case med school, you displace it onto your partner because subconsciously it either feels easier or safer. In this situation, it likely feels easier because your partner is available to you in a tangible way that med school is not.

You may also direct resentment toward your partner because you believe that your undesirable current situation is his fault. You may find yourself saying, "If it wasn't for him, I wouldn't be in this situation in the first place!" I thought this a lot. In these moments it truly feels as though your partner's choices have created the circumstances in your life. This is a defense mechanism called projection.

With projection, we shift our own unacceptable thoughts, feelings, and behaviors onto someone else and respond as if that other person possesses those traits. In our med school relationships, we place the blame on our partner's choices, when in reality we also chose. We were not passive observers in our own lives. We did not go to sleep one night and wake up in a serious relationship with a med student. We played a role and made choices ourselves.

In a moment of my most intense resentment, a very trusted companion said to me, "You may not have chosen med school, but you chose Mike, and you are choosing to stay in these circumstances. You could leave at any time".

She essentially identified my own projection for me. For a little while I disliked her for this, but she was right. Mike was not solely responsible for creating our circumstances. I made a series of choices that led to this point, just as he did.

I thought about what she had said. Yes, I could have left. Many couples live apart for a period of time in their relationships. I could have stayed near or returned to my family. I also could have ended the relationship at any point in time.

When it came down to it, though, I did not like those choices. To be honest, at times I did not like any of my choices, but I preferred to be in the same location as Mike, regardless of med school. I had never really thought about the fact that I had options, and I had certainly never realized that I might actually choose our med school reality above another option.

With projection, you find your own thoughts, feelings, behaviors, and in this case, choices, unsettling. Sure, I might have some legitimate frustration at Mike for his choices, but deep down, my resentment stemmed from the fact that I had also made choices that created this situation. It can feel infuriating and almost intolerable to be upset about your own choices, so the resentment directed at Mike would surface.

As I discussed earlier, I did not know the exact details of med school before entering into this relationship and moving, and at times I felt resentment at having fallen in love and having become invested in this relationship before knowing the whole picture. It was as if I resented the universe for creating my life circumstances this particular way. This was essentially another form of projection where I directed my resentment toward some undefined greater power instead of at my own choices. However, I overlooked two very pertinent realities in thinking this way.

First, Mike also did not know all the exact details of med school before starting. He explained to me in detail what he anticipated, and the rest we had to learn together. Neither of us could anticipate exactly what med school would be, and that is not his fault, just as it is not mine.

Second, none of us know exactly what will happen when we enter into a relationship and make decisions throughout our lives.

We can never know our outcomes beyond a prediction, and Mike and I made our decisions based on predictions, the same way every couple does, regardless of their decisions or circumstances.

This being said, it took me about three years to be able to say! I generally knew in the moment that Mike was not always the correct target for my resentment, but at times I had a difficult time tempering the feelings. That changed over time, and it was a process.

Once I became more aware that Mike did not necessarily deserve my resentment, I mostly moved past the use of displacement and projection. I then found myself cycling between some new defense mechanisms.

When you feel resentment as I have described here, it becomes difficult to simultaneously feel sympathy or closeness toward your partner. Similarly, when you feel connected with your partner, it becomes harder to feel resentful. Because of the requirements of med school, though, you often do not have the time necessary to enjoy your partner and nurture your connection with him. Therefore, you have more of an opportunity for resentment to take hold.

I could recognize that I did not have the time I wanted on a regular basis to nurture my feelings of connection with Mike. I could also recognize that when we did not devote time to our relationship, I started to feel down and then resented Mike. I knew Mike probably did not deserve my resentment, so instead of focusing on the lack of time I had with Mike, I tried to more positively focus on enjoying my independence.

I did things I really liked to do and made plans that Mike did not mind missing. I figured that if I did not focus on the negatives of the situation, I could just live my life as I did when I was single (with some minor exceptions of course!). I have always enjoyed spending time to myself and I know what I like to do, so I just focused on doing my own thing.

Essentially, I was using a defense mechanism called suppression. Suppression involves consciously pushing to the side a feeling or a need in order to cope with the present reality. The intent in suppression is that you will address your feeling or need at a more suitable time, after the difficult moment has passed. Since I could not get my relationship needs met the way I wanted in the present moment, I would push them and the resulting feelings aside until we could better address them.

Unfortunately, reprieve would not come soon enough. I would suppress for so long, waiting for the time when I could better address my feelings and needs, only to find that the time did not come. Predictably, this caused new problems. I found myself getting more and more comfortable in this state of independence until I started to feel new resentments toward Mike.

While trying to postpone the fulfillment of my relationship needs, it started to feel intrusive to still have to address Mike's. While entertaining myself and making my own plans, it became annoying to still be accountable to someone else. I found myself starting to question why, if I have to do everything without Mike, do I still have to be attached to Mike? The relationship started to feel like a nuisance.

*Feeling I could see myself going through.

*Close give me strength + help me to love even when it hurts & I know its going to.

Because I had suppressed my real feelings and relationship needs for an extended period of time, I started operating as if I did not have them. If a person operates as though he does not have relationship needs and relationship oriented feelings for long enough, it becomes very hard to still want to be in a relationship.

As my cycle continued, I caught myself moving past suppression to the unhealthy state of indifference described here. The defense mechanism of passive aggressiveness accompanied the indifference. I became sarcastic and biting toward Mike. I knew I could not reside in this state of indifference and passive aggressiveness for very long before it would become more permanently damaging to our relationship.

In order to erase the feelings of indifference, I found myself going to the opposite extreme. I did anything and everything I could think of to nurture my relationship, even though Mike could not return that same favor. I bought his favorite ice cream, got take out at his favorite restaurant, and did some of his chores around the house.

At that point in time, though, I did not do these things just to be nice. I was compensating for the guilt and fear I felt at having become so indifferent to our relationship. This process of compensation is called reaction formation. Reaction formation occurs when you subconsciously turn your negative or 'dangerous' feelings into their opposites. Instead of feeling resentment, guilt, and uncertainty about our relationship, I did the opposite and nurtured it, gave it all my attention, and smothered it with good feeling and intent.

This helped me feel better for a time. It relieved me of my feelings of guilt and fear. It reminded me that suppression is a coping skill and that I did not truly feel indifferent toward our relationship; I had just tried to temporarily put my relationship needs on hold in order to avoid growing feelings of resentment. I assured myself through this process that I was devoted to our relationship, and I remembered that Mike suffered in the process of med school just as much as I.

This reinvestment in the relationship also reminded me, though, that no matter how much attention I gave to our relationship, it was still only my attention. I remembered again that at the end of the day, I would not have relationship attention returned to me. Eventually, when I had assuaged my guilt and fear, and I tired of lavishing the relationship with unrequited attention, I felt the resentment start to return. I then cycled back into suppression in order to relieve myself of those negative feelings.

I followed this cycle of suppression, passive aggressiveness, and reaction formation for a long time. It became more conscious over time, and I started to gain a better understanding of what I was doing and why I was doing it. After living through this cycle so many times and ultimately gaining this awareness, I moved past these more rudimentary mechanisms and toward healthier ones.

Now, when I do kind things for Mike, I truly want to do something nice, not mask resentment. When I suppress something, I do it only because we need to get through a difficult or stressful moment, and the issue gets addressed as soon as it possibly can. I no longer use these mechanisms to get me through an indefinite period of time.

I have also more consciously chosen to engage in a defense mechanism called sublimation. Sublimation is considered one of the most mature and functional defense mechanisms. It involves transforming negative emotions into positive actions or behaviors. For example, you frequently hear of songwriters turning their intense emotions and difficult experiences into songs. This is sublimation.

As my awareness and understanding of my resentment grew, and I could more reliably place it on the correct target, sometimes Mike, sometimes med school, and sometimes myself, I decided to write a book. I most disliked having free time that I could not spend with Mike, so I decided to channel the emotion I felt at those times into something productive and positive.

When I engaged in suppression, I enjoyed what I did with my free time, but at its deepest level, I did those things in order to avoid other feelings. With sublimation, I do not avoid my feelings; I transform them and channel them into something that not only distracts me, but that I also find truly rewarding. Sublimation can take many forms, and you can find what works for you. You only need a genuine desire to not mask, but transform your resentment into something productive and positive.

You may experience many other defense mechanisms in your quest to manage resentment. Some people try to separate their emotions from their thoughts and intellect, thus engaging in intellectualization. In these situations a person relies on reason and rationalization to explain away feelings because the justification feels easier to accept than the painful emotion. For example, a significant other might find herself saying that she does not mind going to an event alone because then she can socialize with other people more easily, but in reality she is using this justification to push aside the feelings of disappointment or loneliness that she truly experiences.

Some people may find themselves reverting back to earlier developmental stages, such as craving or creating situations in which others have to take care of them. This is regression. In this case, a person may find himself using baby talk, seeking out constant physical comforts, having little tantrums when he does not get his way, or asking others to do things for him that he has already proven he can do on his own. He may also find that responsibilities and tasks that he has managed in the past seem more overwhelming, and he may want to shut down, escape, or seek extra assistance from his partner, parents, or friends.

Others may unknowingly take the resentment inward and experience physical manifestations in illness, headaches, or digestive issues. This is somatization. At times, all of these ailments can stem from legitimate medical issues, but at other times they can also manifest as a symptom of internalized anxiety, depression, and stress. The psyche can use somatization to avoid experiencing the emotional power of these negative feelings since they are instead diverted into the body and experienced physiologically.

*Symptoms to be aware of:
.
o
c
c
o
o
l

These additional mechanisms- intellectualization, regression, and somatization- are less mature mechanisms, as are displacement, projection, passive aggressiveness, and reaction formation. This means that while they may help us to avoid consciously experiencing some negative emotion, they do not actually help us to process or come to terms with the emotion. Further, they can all cause additional problems in our relationships, mental health, and physical health.

Other mature and healthy mechanisms exist in addition to sublimation, and these can start to serve less as defense mechanisms and more as purposeful coping skills. Altruism resembles sublimation in that it transforms the negative feelings into something positive. In the case of altruism, the positive involves serving others in some way. Humor can be a helpful mechanism, and Mike and I use it a great deal when handling our respective difficulties. Anticipation, or planning for future distress, is also a healthier mechanism. This enables you to prepare for an upcoming reality and feel more equipped to handle the predicted feelings.

Suppression is considered a healthier mechanism as well since we often need to put aside a difficult feeling until we can more effectively handle it at a later time. As stated at the beginning of this chapter, though, a defense mechanism becomes a problem when it leads to maladaptive patterns of behavior. As my story illustrates, even a healthy mechanism can lead to maladaptive patterns, as suppression did for me at times. These healthier mechanisms only remain healthy if they truly transform the underlying emotion and not simply mask it.

Conclusion

This chapter has described my journey with resentment through the times of med school overwhelm. I certainly do not suggest that everyone will encounter the same journey. Everyone's story is different, and each med school experience and relationship is unique in some way.

However, everyone that I have met with a partner in med school has eventually experienced some amount of resentment, and it can be extremely difficult to overcome. You need to accept your own role in the choices you have made and the lack of impact your med student has over the realities of med school. You also have to try to understand your method of managing resentment and make it more conscious and healthy over time. Until you do all this, you will find resentment coming in and out of your life.

Acceptance is the hardest part. It took me a long time to feel ready to relinquish the role of 'victim to med school'. I found it so gratifying to complain about med school and blame it for everything that happened in my life. It is much easier to be mad at something else for changing your life than it is to acknowledge that you have chosen to feel like a victim. Will the realities of med school magically change when you release this role? No. But once you decide you want to move past this state and feel in control of your own life again, it becomes much easier to manage it all.

Part Three
Working Through

6

Components Of A
Successful Med School
Relationship

For the purposes of this book, I am defining a 'successful relationship' as a relationship that lasts over time with two happy and trusting members. The details within the relationship only need to work for both members. I do not write with any judgment about the decisions made, content agreed upon, or direction taken within your relationships. The characteristics explored in this chapter and the following chapters are based on broad concepts I have seen in the med school relationships that last over time with two happy and trusting members. I do not seek to tell anyone what the intimate details of your relationship should entail. I simply point out the general concepts that I have seen in many 'successful' med school relationships.

A successful relationship does not exist without effort. Like a plant, a relationship requires the fulfillment of certain basic needs in order to thrive. A plant first needs a foundation. It needs the ground cleared and its seeds planted. In order to grow it requires water, sunlight, and weeding. Once it flowers, it needs to be pruned and maintained.

A successful relationship also needs tending at these different levels. It requires a foundation, nurturance to grow, and ongoing maintenance. If you believe that your relationship is succeeding without these components, it means one of two things. Either your relationship is less stable than you think it is, and it will struggle when actually tested, or your partner does all of the maintenance work for you both. I have referred to the latter phenomenon as one-sided emotion work, and from this point on, we will explore the process of changing your relationship back to more typical, two-sided emotion work where both partners engage in relationship maintenance together.

Members of any relationship need to possess a certain set of skills and qualities in order for that relationship to be successful. These tend to involve characteristics that aid in communication, compassion, compromise, and conflict resolution. Everyone may not innately possess these characteristics. Fortunately, they do not need to come naturally as we can develop them over time.

A med school relationship requires the presence of these relationship skills, and it also requires some additional skills and qualities as well. Members of a med school relationship do not need to possess all of the characteristics that I will describe here, but the presence of at least some of these traits in your relationship will help. Again, these skills do not have to come naturally to you or your partner since they can grow and develop as you practice them in your relationship over time.

Through this chapter I will explore three categories of characteristics that can help your med school relationship: those in the significant other, those in the med student, and those in your relationship as a whole. I will then explore in more detail some of the more universal and important characteristics in the following chapters.

Characteristics of the Significant Other

During the stressful periods of med school, a significant other will generally have a great deal of time without her med student and be responsible for much of the work that occurs within the relationship. During these times, the significant other will likely not get back in return the same amount of support and energy that she gives.

Because of this, as a successful significant other, you will either already possess or need to develop a well of patience, independence, and emotional strength. You will need a strong sense of the big picture and of the long-term goals toward which you and your partner are working. You will also want to cultivate a strong sense of self and confidence so as not to take personally the moments when you experience time alone and a lack of support.

You will need a support system available. You will need people with whom to talk and do things. You will need these people to help you get your own emotion needs met since your med student will not always be able to do that for you.

As much as you will need other people, they will also be unavailable to you at times. Because of this, you will likely find it beneficial to not only do things by yourself but also enjoy doing them by yourself. This will come naturally to some but not to others. Take this opportunity to develop this skill because using and enjoying your independence can help a great deal during this time. Enjoying your time to yourself can be the difference between just getting through this difficult time and truly continuing to live and cultivate your life. Many significant others take this time to pursue their own dreams and goals while they have the time and independence within their relationship to do so.

You will need coping skills. You will need to know what to do when you are sad, stressed, mad, scared, lonely, and tired. You will need to know what will help you get through a bad day, week, or month. You can expect moments of support from your med student, but during times of overwhelm, you may find that you largely need to work through your difficult times without him. Know what makes you feel better, gives you release, distracts you in a healthy way, and calms you down. You will need these tools regularly.

As a successful significant other, you will need to show your med student a great deal of support. You will likely have the more difficult position in the relationship, but during times of overwhelm, your med student likely has the more difficult day-to-day job. Sometimes this is not the case, and eventually this shifts to a more equal balance in your relationship. However, when your med student is adjusting to and moving through the most difficult parts of med school, he generally has the more demanding daily tasks, and you generally have the more demanding role in the relationship. As your med student's daily tasks become less overwhelming, you will likely see that your role in the relationship becomes less challenging as well.

Perhaps one of your two hardest tasks as a successful significant other is finding the balance between taking care of yourself and nurturing your relationship. It can be difficult to know that you need to occupy yourself and take care of your own needs and at the same time still feel an investment in your relationship. It is difficult to meet someone's needs every day without getting yours met to the same extent by that person in return. To survive this, you will find ways to get your needs met. However, if you take this too far, you risk losing your investment in your relationship or feeling like the relationship is no longer necessary. You risk feeling annoyed, irritated, and most dangerously, resentful. Because of this, you need to find a balance between taking care of yourself and still nurturing your relationship. You also do not carry full responsibility for this, and I will discuss that momentarily.

The second of your hardest tasks as a successful significant other is finding and maintaining a state of acceptance: acceptance of the choices you and your med student have made, of the process of med school, of the reality in which you exist, of the losses this brings, of your commitment to one another, and of the reasons you made this choice in the first place.

Acceptance is probably the most important quality that a significant other can bring to the relationship because it limits resentment, and resentment has the power to destroy your relationship if left unchecked for too long.

Characteristics of the Med Student

Med students, I will start with the two most important qualities that you can bring to your relationship. The first is a commitment to making and keeping your relationship a high priority. If you want your relationship to succeed, you need to make it your top priority when med school does not need to be. Your relationship has to rank highest when you do not have a medicine related commitment. That does not mean you do not maintain friendships, family relationships, or hobbies. It simply means that you give your relationship attention first, and you ensure that your relationship is healthy and intact before you turn your attention to anything else.

The second most important quality you can bring to your relationship is a willingness to move toward a more equal balance of responsibility in the relationship. No one expects that this will happen while you still experience the most difficult parts of med school. Once you start to move through these difficult times, though, it is important for you to be willing to work toward a healthier long-term balance in your relationship. Your ability to do this will increase with time, and as it does, you will need to make a concentrated effort to re-balance the roles, responsibilities, and emotion work that occur in your relationship. This willingness alone is one of the most important characteristics of a med student in a successful relationship.

As a med student in a successful relationship, you will need to find a balance, over time, between school and the rest of your life. This can be extremely hard to do, but with practice it is possible. In order to develop this balance, you will need to find a way to stop thinking about what you are studying or what happened in your day in order to give your significant other your undivided attention. Your partner will not always want to hear about the neuro-pathways that you are studying, and she will likely want to tell you about things that happened in her day as well. Find time to shut off the medicine part of your brain and turn on the part that pays attention to your partner. A little attention can go a long way.

While you listen to your significant other, you, as a med student in a successful relationship, need to hear and try to understand her reality. It may not seem as significant or intense or awful as yours feels to you, but in reality you do not know what it feels like to be in her position. You do not want her to belittle your experiences and reality, and you cannot belittle hers. You both make sacrifices along this journey. It may look at times on the surface as though your significant other has no trouble and gets to do whatever she wants. However, at least a portion of what your significant other does with her time is likely designed to make up for what she temporarily does not get from the relationship. If you find yourself having a hard time sympathizing with your partner's situation, it also may help to remember that you have your partner to lean on when you have a hard time or need support, but your partner likely needs to get that support elsewhere, at least some of the time.

For at least a portion of med school, you will likely have very little time to give to your significant other. As a med student in a successful relationship, though, you will need to try to find a way to ensure that you and your partner spend time together. This may involve taking study breaks at specific or strategic times. It may mean planning certain activities that you ensure you do together such as meals, TV shows, conversations, or bedtime routines. It may involve picking one weekend night a week when you do not study, or one day a month when you do nothing school related. There is no correct way to make this happen, but you and your partner need to coordinate schedules and find time to see one another. You cannot have a successful relationship with someone you never see or speak to.

Additionally, you will need to help your significant other get her needs met whenever you can. I will explore this more in the next chapter, but essentially, whatever your significant other misses the most when you are unavailable to her is what you need to attempt to do when you have some time to invest in your relationship. This may involve doing housework, talking, taking a walk, engaging in an activity, physical intimacy, etc. Provide her with what she needs when you have the opportunity because there will be periods of time when she largely has to take care of those needs on her own.

Lastly, as much as you can during this difficult time, you need to remain a whole and complete person. A successful and healthy relationship can only occur with two whole and healthy people, so this means you need to remain whole and healthy. Of course medicine will take over at times, and at times you will only be able to access that part of yourself. However, you cannot lose the rest of what makes you who you are. As best you can, continue to develop your non-medical interests and hobbies. Do not let your non-medical relationships fall apart. Remember the traits you possess that you and others value in you, and cultivate these as much as possible. Do this for your significant other who fell in love with all of you, not just the medical part of you, but also do this for yourself so that you can continue to live a well-rounded life.

Characteristics of the Relationship

While each individual may not necessarily need to possess all the qualities described above (though it can certainly help!), I do think that the following all exist in a successful long-term med school relationship. I have not seen a successful med school relationship that is missing one of these qualities. These characteristics do not present in all relationships from the start, but they can develop over time. Additionally, these characteristics have specific applications to med school re-lationships, but they also exist in successful relationships in general.

Perhaps most importantly, both partners need to make the commitment to make it through together. A relationship will only last through the difficult times if both partners have made the decision ahead of time that they will not leave during the difficult times. If one person has reservations about staying in the relationship regardless of what circumstances occur, then at some point there will be a set of circumstances that will seem 'bad enough' to make that person decide to leave. Med school will provide you with plenty of circumstances that feel 'bad enough', so unless you have made the commitment to make it through together, there is definite possibility that you will not.

Also of importance, both members of the relationship need to have the same big picture vision and set of priorities for your life. I will address this in detail in the next chapter, but for now suffice it to say that if both partners do not prioritize the relationship in the same way, medicine will have ample opportunity to take over. The nature of medicine can be all encompassing, especially during the education and training process and especially if one lets it. If you do not have a clear and agreed upon expectation about where your relationship ranks in relation to medicine and what you will and will not sacrifice in the name of medicine, then medicine can easily infiltrate and take over.

Communication between partners is essential. You each live such different realities produced by the same set of circumstances. At times you may find yourself assuming you know what your partner experiences because you encounter the same circumstances. At other times you may feel as though you have no idea what happens with your partner since you have such different experiences within your circumstances. You are joined to one another while you go through the medicine process, and you can only empathize with your partner and stay committed to the same end goals by communicating along the way.

Both partners need to listen to one another and respect and value the other's reality. Through this kind of communication, both partners can learn the needs of the other and then try to meet as many of those as possible. You both need to commit to making each other's lives better and easier so that as this journey progresses, you both still feel invested and want the relationship to last. If a relationship does not receive attention and effort from both partners, it will eventually fall into ruin. If both partners truly respect and regard the experiences of the other, though, it becomes much easier for that relationship to stand strong. You need to have sympathy and understanding on both sides, and neither partner can take the other for granted.

Lastly, you and your partner need to make sure you have a way of staying connected when time, energy, and emotional stores run low. The method of connecting will vary depending on the couple, but talking, physical contact, humor, and general idiosyncrasies can all help couples to feel connected without having to invest much time, energy, and emotion.

The components of a successful med school relationship that I have listed here are actually fairly complex ideas, and I will explore many of them in more detail over the next several chapters.

7

Priorities, Realities, And Compromises

The previous chapter outlined some general characteristics of a successful med school relationship. This chapter will explore some of those components in more detail as well as offer some tools and strategies that can help to cultivate these characteristics in your own relationships.

We all have our own set of priorities in life. Priorities are the aspects of our lives that we value as the most important. Generally speaking, we seek to act in a way that promotes our priorities and live in accordance with what we deem to be important. We hope that the reality of our lives, or the actual circumstances, abilities, and limitations that we encounter, encourages our priorities.

Sometimes, though, the realities can make it difficult to live by our priorities. When this happens, we find ourselves needing to compromise. We need to find a way to bridge the opposing forces we have met. We want our values to be central in the actuality of our existence, and at times this will involve some negotiation or compromise with the realities that we face.

At times the realities that challenge the implementation of our priorities occur within our individual lives. We may be asked to make commitments at work that would cause our self-care to suffer. We may find ourselves deciding between career and family or financial stability and emotional stability. We may face changes in our circumstances that necessitate a change in the way we have previously enacted our priorities.

At other times occurrences within our relationships may challenge the implementation of our priorities. Both members in a relationship have their own set of priorities. Sometimes these work in conjunction with one another and sometimes they do not. This chapter will address both the relational and circumstantial realities that can impact the actualization of priorities.

This process is important for all people in their own lives as well as for members of any relationship. Portions of this chapter will make sense for any couple trying to address these issues. However, we will also look specifically at how med school impacts this process and the tools you can use to address this impact.

Identifying Needs

Priorities are based on needs, desires, and values. Before you can prioritize and compromise, you have to be aware of each of these components in your own life. They occur at many levels and permeate all aspects of your life.

You need to know what you hope and want from your life in general. These are your long-term dreams and your big picture values. How will you know if your life is a success? What do you value? What makes your life feel complete? What can you not live without? What do you want to accomplish? What will make you happy over the course of your life?

You will have smaller scale and shorter-term hopes and plans. These may involve more current goals for careers, relationships, families, finances, and possessions. What do you want from each of these areas? What balance do you want between them? What role will your career play in your life? How will you know your career is a good match for you? What role will your relationships play in your life? What do you expect from your relationships?

You will also have your day-to-day preferences. What do you want your day-to-day existence to look like? What kind of routine are you comfortable with? Who is involved in your day-to-day life? How do you want to use your time on a daily basis? What is necessary for you to regularly feel happy?

All of these needs, desires, and values indicate what is important to you in these different areas of your life, and they comprise your set of priorities. We will now look at these levels of priorities as they pertain to relationships, particularly med school relationships.

Big Picture Priorities

The most fundamental priorities are those that address your basic life goals and values. They encompass the big picture, and they describe what you want out of your life as a whole. Often these priorities serve as a foundation for relationships. People are drawn together for a variety of reasons, but people with similar big picture priorities will often find it easier to stay together. When members of a relationship agree about their lives' values and direction, they can then work toward the same ultimate goal. They will have disagreements and conflicts along the way, but it becomes easier to negotiate and compromise on the smaller details when they have the same ultimate goal in mind.

I cannot tell you what your big picture priorities are or should be. I assume, though, that since you are reading this book, you are attempting to make a committed relationship work during med school, and I can tell you that the successful med school couples I know have made it their goal to make their relationship the top priority as often as they can.

In your med school relationship, you will likely struggle with priorities at some point. Medicine and the relationship will both vie for first priority. Sometimes a med student has very little control over medicine being the first priority, and at times med school will require your energy and resources at the expense of your relationship getting those resources. At other times, particularly as the periods of overwhelm decrease, it becomes easier for the relationship to come first. In the end, your relationship has a much greater chance of success if med school only takes the position of first priority when it absolutely has to.

Some people have a difficult time setting this priority. Some med students feel that medicine should always come first. I have heard people issue the argument that as a doctor, their job is "a matter of life and death" and therefore nothing can come before it. If you find this notion present in your relationship, I offer some considerations.

First, it is certainly true that at times medicine is a "matter of life and death", and while a doctor is at work dealing with those matters of life and death, I truly hope that nothing else comes first above doing the job well. However, generally speaking, more than one doctor occupies an area, and more than one person has the skill set necessary to address those matters of life and death. Another doctor will take the next shift or the next case, and he can deal with the life and death matters for that shift or for that patient. I do acknowledge that some specialties create such highly specialized positions that this argument may not be as true. However, this brings me to my second point.

Both partners in your relationship have made choices. Significant other, you chose to be in a relationship with a person impacted by medicine, and therefore you have to accept certain realities. However, med student, you also chose to be in a relationship while being in medicine, and therefore you have to accept certain realities as well.

I understand that your dream of medicine may have existed longer than your relationship has, and some people use this as an explanation for why they then should avoid doing anything to 'compromise' that dream. Med student, at some point you will need to decide how important it is to have your significant other in your life. If you decide you truly want her in your life and that having her in your life is a priority, then you will need to find a way to incorporate both her and medicine into your life in a manner that both you and your partner can accept.

Med student, you have not chosen to do medicine alone; you have chosen to do it while in a relationship. This means that while your significant other makes sacrifices and compromises in her life to accommodate your career path, you need to compromise in order to accommodate your relationship. In the bigger picture, you need to decide as a couple if your relationship is going to be as important as "matters of life and death". Will medicine always come first, or will your relationship come first with only moments when medicine needs to come first?

If your goal is different than putting your relationship first when possible and medicine first when necessary, then you need to be certain that you both find this goal truly acceptable. Both members of a relationship can agree to a different set of big picture priorities than that presented here and still have a successful relationship. However, you need to agree on your set of priorities. The strength of the foundation upon which you will build the rest of your lives together depends on your level of agreement about your big picture priorities. If you agree about these, then you are starting with a strong foundation. If you do not, then all other trials in your relationship will ultimately come back to this fundamental disagreement.

Smaller Scale Priorities

With your long-term needs identified and your big picture priorities agreed upon, you have set a strong foundation for yourselves and your relationship. You will have day-to-day squabbles and disagreements, and you will find a give and take in your daily routines. With your long-term goals, values, and priorities established, though, it becomes easier to compromise and work through these more quotidian differences.

Based on the values you have identified, you will start to see what you need in your everyday life. Do you crave routine, structure, and consistency? Do you want excitement and novel encounters? Do you want alone time, time together, some of each? What do you want to fit into your day, your week, or your month? What role do you want your partner to play in that? There are many questions to consider, and you and your partner will likely experience at least some differences in your day-to-day preferences. There is no one best way to structure your daily existence and no best set of priorities to consider. You will both need to learn each other's preferences in order to make your daily life work in a way that grants you both as much contentment as possible.

Further, you will need to continue to assess and evaluate your day-to-day preferences and needs as med school progresses. A med student will find needs during med school that did not exist before. He will develop new habits and learn new ways of studying. He will have new peers, new routines, new time commitments, and new environments. He will need different kinds of communication and support. His emotional, physical, and logistical needs will change.

Similarly, significant others, you will find changes in your needs. As your partner's needs, emotional and physical availability, peer groups, and routines all change, you will need to assess how this impacts and changes what you require on a daily basis. You will find yourself re-prioritizing your previous needs. Some will become less important and others may feel more intense.

This process is very unique to each couple since your daily priorities are so specific to each of you as individuals. However, in order to maintain the health and ultimate success of your relationship, it is important that you both commit to this one smaller scale, day-to-day priority; you both need to try to ensure that your partner regularly feels loved and valued in your relationship. It will become significantly easier to find a way to figure out all of the other logistics in your relationship if you both feel connected to, loved by, valued by, and appreciated by the other. I am going to introduce a concept here that can help ensure that you each meet this one, very important, smaller scale priority.

Communicating Love to Your Partner

We all experience love differently. Many books, conversations, and debates have explored the ways that people express and receive love. These often attempt to make a distinction along gender lines, indicating that women and men communicate and experience love in different ways. Some broad generalizations likely exist between men and women, but much more importantly and superseding any gender divide remains the fact that every individual experiences love in his or her own unique way.

What do we mean by expressing and receiving love? Expressing love has to do with the way we demonstrate our feelings of love to someone. For example, a person might try to do nice things for his partner, provide her with gifts or tokens of his thought, or give her his undivided attention when she wants to talk. Receiving love has to do with how we interpret the loving actions of others and how those specific actions make us feel. A person may feel most loved when spending quality time with her partner, cuddling with her partner, or hearing encouragement from her partner.

We all naturally express and receive love in different ways. Therefore, it is very likely that you and your partner do this differently. Perhaps one partner shows love by trying to help out around the house, but the other feels love when her partner cuddles with her and talks about her day. In this situation, the second partner may experience fewer loving feelings, not due to lack of effort by her partner, but because she has a harder time receiving his expression of love.

It becomes important to understand the different ways that both you and your partner more naturally communicate and experience love. This allows you both to better express your love to one another as well as have it more effectively received.

We tend to show love to others in a form that is easiest for us to receive. This has significance for two reasons. First, we can find clues about how our partners receive love through the way they show us love. Second, we need to understand that at times our partner may attempt to express love, but we miss it since it has come in a form that feels less natural for us.

These considerations are important while you try to distinguish the patterns of expressing and receiving love in your relationship. In the end, though, we have a responsibility to our partners to express love to them in a way that feels more natural to them and that is easiest for them to receive. Your partner can then more naturally accept and experience your expression of love. This will leave you both feeling more fulfilled, connected, and loved within your relationship.

In our example above, the partner who more naturally shows love by helping out around the house needs to make an effort to cuddle with his partner and talk to her about her day so that she has the opportunity to more naturally experience his feelings of love for her. In return, she cannot just cuddle with and talk to him and think this sufficiently communicates her love for him. This is how she most readily feels love, and she needs to show him love in a way that is easiest for him to receive, whatever that may be.

I mention this concept here as a tool that you and your partner can use on a daily basis to ensure that your relationship remains a priority. Using these techniques is not overly difficult or time consuming, yet it can go a long way in making you and your partner feel more connected, even during difficult or trying times. When you add this more routine relationship maintenance to your already solid foundation of agreed upon big picture priorities, you further develop a healthy and successful relationship.

Learning to Compromise Within the Realities of Med School

With big picture priorities settled and a commitment in place to trying to make the other feel loved and valued, all that remains is negotiating the logistical items that emerge every day.

Everyone has heard and used the word compromise. We do this routinely as we navigate our day. We do it with family, significant others, friends, co-workers, clients, and even with ourselves. Rarely do we get something exactly as we envisioned it to be, and that is okay. We look for a reasonable approximation, and we continue on.

When we think of compromise in a traditional way, we conceptualize this:

```
    Person 1                        Person 2
   A--------------------> C <----------------------B
```

In this diagram, Person 1 and Person 2 each stand on one side of a conflict- Person 1 at Point A and Person 2 at Point B. They each concede part of their original position and meet in the middle at Point C (for compromise!). Each side has made a concession for the greater good of finding a solution.

Compromising with med school is a little trickier. I conceptualize compromising during times of med school overwhelm like this:

```
            Person 1                        Person 2
   0-------------------> A--------------------> C <-------------------B
```

In this diagram, we still have Person 1 and Person 2 standing at different points in a conflict (Point A and Point B) and meeting at Point C for their solution to the current situation. However, this diagram includes something else. You can see here that in reality, Point C is not actually in the middle. Person 1 does not begin at her original starting point, Point O. In fact, Person 1 has already compromised from her original starting point at Point O all the way to Point A. Then from Point A, she and Person 2 try to find a compromise between Point A and Point B.

This represents compromising during the most difficult and stressful times of med school overwhelm. It also represents one-sided emotion work. Significant other, I am sure you can guess by now that you are Person 1.

Compromising becomes tricky in our med school relationships because we have three entities in our relationship instead of the more typical two. Med school is an entity in our relationships, and it comes with the inability to compromise. During those times when your med student is inextricably linked to med school, his portion of the relationship and relationship resources becomes much less flexible. Only the significant other and her resources maintain any flexibility during those moments. Because of this, you will likely find yourself in the kind of compromise situation presented above.

However, at some point you will want to start moving past this.

Everything about med school is a process, and this is no exception. Moving into a new form of compromising will take time and is in and of itself a compromise. It takes commitment from both partners. You will need to remember that you are in this together and are working together toward your same big picture goals.

Med students, you will need to start returning to your partner the emotional support she gives to you. First, and most simply, you need to take advantage of your free time. I know you do not have much of it, but depending on your school's curriculum and your particular strengths, there will be times you have more of it than at others. Many students find they have more time once rotations start, but again this depends on your personal strengths.

You need to learn to recognize when you have a period of low stress and when you can afford to take time off, whether that be an hour, a night, or a weekend. You need to recognize that even though your significant other does not do your school work or work your long hours, she does and manages so many other things that accommodate you. When you have time off or less stress, repay your significant other. Do whatever it is that makes you two feel close and that makes your significant other feel loved.

Significant other, you also need to use these times strategically. We have discussed how you accommodate many things during med school. If you can recognize, though, when your med student is in a good mood, moving less frantically, and talking and engaging with you longer, you can use these times to recharge yourself and get your needs met. Address the topics that have remained unaddressed. Ask your questions, call in your favors, and make your plans. Settle the unsettled. Also, do the things you miss doing with your med student. During these times have fun, laugh, and enjoy one another.

These low stress periods will not necessarily happen in a predictable pattern. Use them, though, to remember why you and your partner like one another because at times you will forget and need reminding. Med student, if you can use your words and actions to remind your significant other about the good in your relationship, it will increase your significant other's desire to support you when you are stressed and busy. If you can both remember the ways your partner naturally receives love, it will allow you both to make your partner feel loved with minimal intervention and energy.

This entire process is a form of compromise. Significant other, you work hard for your med student when your med student is stressed and unavailable. Med student, you work hard for your significant other when you have the capacity to do so. You both show your hard work and commitment to the other by expressing your love in a way the other can more naturally receive.

Putting it all Together
Ultimately, the content of your compromises depends on your priorities. Ideally, your big picture priorities are secure, and you are working to manage your day-to-day priorities. If this daily management includes an understanding of the ways you communicate love to one another, then you can significantly decrease the distress of any remaining conflicts.

Areas that do cause distress require compromise. These areas will be different for each individual and each relationship. Circumstances in your relationship that feel healthy and normal might cause distress for another individual or another couple. Similarly, other couples may handle certain experiences with ease while they prove more problematic for your relationship. These differences are normal, and the content of your conflicts and compromises will be based on the unique priorities and needs within your relationship.

While the content of your compromises depends on your priorities and needs, how you compromise depends on the stage of your personal med school experience. During the times of overwhelm, you will likely find yourselves compromising in a way consistent with the second diagram in this chapter. Med student moves from Point B to Point C, and significant other looks like she moves from Point A to Point C but in reality she started at Point O.

As you start to incorporate the themes from this chapter into your relationship, you will find that Point C starts to move more evenly between Point B and Point O until eventually your compromising process resembles the first diagram. The strategies described in this chapter are designed to help this shift start to occur. In Part Four, we will look at how this process ultimately completes and returns more fully to an equal balance.

Like all couples on this journey, Mike and I moved through these stages. We agreed about our big picture priorities from the start; we both value our careers and the paths we are taking as individuals, but we also want a relationship and a family in which we both participate and enjoy. We had a strong understanding of our more daily needs prior to med school starting, but we learned a great deal more about these needs as we moved through med school and they started changing. Expressing our love for one another in ways the other could receive helped us to connect when time was at a premium. It enabled us to more purposefully express and experience our feelings and sustain our relationship.

I experience love primarily through quality time spent together as well as through physical connection. Quality time can be difficult to create with the time constraints of med school, but we negotiated some compromises. We tried to find smaller versions of what I desired in order to try to meet this need. I could not have a great deal of quality time every day with Mike, but he remembered that I primarily feel love this way, and he would make an effort whenever he could. Over time, we started having more time together again, and it became easier to do this more completely.

We also grew to supplement with more physical connection. I was able to forgo a great deal of the quality time I initially missed when we increased our physical contact, especially our fleeting and momentary physical contact. This helped us a great deal. Physical contact requires much less time and energy, and so it evolved into a primary way for us to feel connected.

Mike felt that growing up he primarily received love through words of encouragement and verbal praise, but since starting med school, he found that this had changed. He started to feel love more readily when I helped him with some task or brought him some tangible token or 'gift' when I returned home after being out. Due to our circumstances, it started to feel like an act of good faith and love when I did something for him that he did not have the time to do himself or when I brought him home some symbolic gesture of my thoughts for him while we had been doing separate things.

Just having an awareness of these concepts helped us to better identify the intent behind the things we each did for one another. This created a sense of appreciation that is necessary in a relationship with limited resources. It also helped us to know what actions were unnecessary, so neither of us used our limited energy engaging in tasks that had no meaning to the other.

Additionally, these concepts helped us to match our priorities with our realities. By learning to interpret one another's acts of love, and then practicing this over time, we found ways to make our relationship feel as though it was not always second to med school. Our relationship more consistently felt like a top priority since tending to it felt more effortless and happened with more regularity. It became easier to accept those moments when med school had to take first priority, knowing that it was only temporary and that we would still maintain the relationship.

As every couple does, we had our logistical issues to work through and our topics that required compromises. Some of our compromises along the way have come from learning to communicate within the realities of our relationship, and I will explore this more in the next chapter.

You will find a time in this med school process when your med student starts to become more available again. When this happens, it is time to start shifting the balance of emotion work and compromise back to a more equal place. It makes sense to use one-sided emotion work and manage temporarily, even if that lasts a couple years, but eventually you want to move beyond a healthy med school relationship and grow into a healthy relationship in general. This starts to happen when you both have your relationship needs met a more equal amount of the time.

You will also see, over time, that med school starts to take up less than one third of your relationship resources. When you learn to support one another more equally on this journey and you have moments of more complete team work, med school loses its grip. It still always has a place in your relationship, and there will always be times it requires the attention and resources in your relationship, but over time it will take a smaller portion of those resources. As you and your partner move forward on this journey together, your relationship will grow and strengthen as well. When you trust that you will both take care of your relationship together, it makes giving resources to med school much less painful.

I will discuss the completion of this transition in Part Four. For now we will continue to explore other helpful perspectives, tools, and strategies to use along the way.

8

Communication

In order to apply many of the concepts discussed in the previous chapters, you will need to be able to communicate with your partner. The need for and the principles of communicating in a med school relationship do not differ greatly from those present in a non-med school relationship. Because of that, I will briefly highlight some general principles of communicating in a relationship and then address a few that seem to emerge more frequently or play a greater role in a med school relationship.

General Communication Skills

The biggest part of communicating is listening. Listening means not only hearing words and sounds but ideas and meaning as well. Listening cannot occur when a person is planning his next statement or comeback. Listening does not happen when a person thinks he already knows what his partner is going to say next. In those cases, a person only hears what he thinks he is going to hear, not what is actually said.

Good listening only happens when a person thinks about the speaker, the context for the current situation, and the significance that this situation has for the speaker. Good listening cannot occur when a person only thinks about the impact the speaker's words have on himself. Good listening involves hearing feelings and meaning as well as just words.

In order to ensure that a person has listened well and heard correctly, it can be useful for that person to summarize what he heard and reflect this back to the speaker. This can feel silly sometimes, but it serves to ensure that this person has heard and interpreted correctly. It also helps the speaker to know that he was heard as well.

When communicating, it is important to speak in such a way that makes the other person want to listen. This involves using factual statements that do not place blame on the listener. A statement such as, "I feel lonely when you study at night" is significantly different from, "You never want to spend time with me". In the first, the speaker takes responsibility for her own feelings and states a fact to the listener. In this case, the listener is much more likely to respond in a sympathetic and helpful manner than if the speaker used the latter statement, which sounds blaming and provokes defensiveness.

It is also important when communicating for a person's verbal and non-verbal messages to be the same. When a person sits down with open body language and eye contact and says, "Tell me about your day", it is very different from a person who says it while walking into the other room opening the mail or while turning up the volume on the TV.

A person's non-verbal and verbal messages can only synchronize, though, if the verbal messages make sense and are clear themselves. The speaker must say what she means to say. The listener is not, nor should he be, able to read the speaker's mind. The speaker needs to ask a question if she wants an answer or make a suggestion if she wants something done. The only way to know what someone is thinking is for that person to say it aloud. Wanting the listener to guess a meaning or offer comment without the speaker having stated her actual intent is futile, time consuming, and unnecessary. Communicating is significantly easier without games and guesswork.

A good rule of thumb is to communicate with your partner the way you want your partner to communicate with you. If you want your partner to listen unconditionally to you when you have something to talk about, you better be prepared to do the same for your partner. If you want your partner to actually hear the meaning in what you say, you need to hear the meaning in what your partner says. It goes both ways, and it is safe to say that you cannot expect more than what you are willing to give yourself.

Communication in Med School
As I said, the concepts and skills used for effective communication are the same regardless of the presence of med school. However, some communication principles become particularly important when med school is involved. All of the skills discussed in this section can help in other relationships and in other forms of communicating as well, but they are especially important while communicating within your med school relationship.

Possibly the hardest part about communicating during med school is the presence of significant time constraints. Logistically, your med student does not have much free time. Emotionally, he has even less availability. Over time, you will need to figure out how to fit in communicating.

For the first couple years of med school when we experienced the most intense moments of med school overwhelm, Mike and I reached the arrangement that we would talk about day-to-day matters if either of us really wanted or needed to or if we had to make plans or decisions. We would talk primarily at dinner because we shared that time together. Topics that did not require immediate attention but that still needed to be addressed in a fairly timely manner, I would save until after he completed an exam or for a time when he was just generally not as busy. Topics or issues that were not time sensitive but that involved the growth and adjustment of our relationship tended to wait until a semester break because then Mike could give them much more of his attention, and I felt heard and valued. This arrangement would certainly not work for everyone, and you will need to find an arrangement that works for you as a couple. You will need to find something that works, though, because with med school, communicating effortlessly will not always happen.

At times issues or topics may grow out of proportion due to a lack of time to discuss them. We had to learn that some topics I could not keep to myself until a more convenient time because I could not prevent them from escalating in my head. In those cases, we learned that it was far better for our relationship if I raised the issue and addressed it immediately, even if it was not the most convenient time for Mike. If I did not, we would end up in an argument two weeks later that was so out of proportion to the original topic that it nullified the benefit of waiting for a convenient time. You will need to decide in your own relationship how to manage this, but if you feel something erupting to a size it should not or need not have, you need to address it before it gets worse, even if that means discussing it at a less convenient time.

It is also important to make sure you communicate when you feel disconnected from your partner. An unavoidable level of separation occurs with med school, and you will need to use all your tools and skills to manage this. However, this level of separation is different from a true feeling of disconnect. The separation is physical and logistical, and it occurs due to a lack of free time and competing commitments. Disconnect is characterized by questioning the value you place on the relationship, having a difficult time feeling any compassion for your partner's situation or for your partner in general, and feeling burdened by your responsibility and accountability to your partner. This kind of disconnect requires a reconnection in order to keep the relationship in a healthy state.

Sometimes just having a meaningful conversation with your partner about anything will remove that disconnect. Sometimes you will need to explain your disconnected feeling and what you need in order to feel reconnected. Often just having this conversation and knowing your partner now knows how you feel can restore that connection. Other times you may need to take some time together and foster the reconnection more purposefully.

Significant other, you will also need to communicate if you find yourself feeling unappreciated, underappreciated, or condescended to in any way. As discussed earlier, med students can get caught up in the difficulty and intensity of what they do every day, and sometimes this results in a lack of compassion for anyone or anything that they view as less intense. It makes sense that they may get caught up in this feeling, but it is not okay for them to truly mean it and hold it over you.

You may or may not address this issue in the moment that it occurs. Some people prefer to know your reaction immediately and can understand your position and integrate this information quickly. Other people receive feedback more effectively once the intense moment has passed. You will need to figure this out as it applies to your relationship and make your decisions accordingly. Regardless, though, of when you address this issue, it does need to be addressed, particularly if it recurs.

Lastly, it is important to find a balance between ensuring that a significant other is heard and understood and that the med student does not experience excessive guilt. Med students can feel very guilty and responsible for a significant other's unhappiness or disappointment with the med school process. They know that their significant other encounters these experiences because they chose this career path.

As a significant other, it can feel vindicating at times to know that your partner knows enough about your experiences to feel bad for this situation. We cannot forget, though, that they did not actually put us in this situation. It is true that you would not be in this situation if your med student did not attend med school, but you chose to be in and stay in this relationship regardless. As we have already concluded, you could leave at any point, and yet you have not. Because of this, we need to be careful to make ourselves heard and understood without intensifying the med student's guilt or sense of responsibility. It is not fair to put onto your partner your own active daily choice to stay.

It certainly becomes easier to make yourself understood without fostering guilt in your med student when your med student is willing to hear you and accept your reality. Med student, it is when you send the advertent or inadvertent message that you do not believe her reality that she may then find herself ready to defend 'just how bad it really is'. You may not want to face this reality because it may provoke feelings of guilt in you. However, you will have to find a way to understand that your denial or dismissal of your partner's reality can evoke in her the fighting desire to defend her reality without regard for managing your sense of guilt.

Med student, you are not responsible for your significant other's choices. She makes her choice every day to stay and be a part of this relationship, even knowing what she knows now. She needs to share her reality with you, though. She should not try to blame you or make you feel bad; she simply needs to communicate with you so she can feel connected to you. You will likely share your reality with her on a daily basis, so it is only fair that you know and understand her reality as well. This is an important balance for both of you to find so that you can communicate with one another and have a true appreciation for each other's positions. Without this it becomes much more difficult to move forward together.

Reaching this level of communication and understanding will take time. Like everything in this book, it is a process, and making progress in this area will help you to move toward a more permanent positive shift in your relationship.

9

Cultivating Support

I have talked at length in the last three chapters about the roles and responsibilities of both partners with regard to the work phase of a med school relationship. Both partners play a role in moving away from the difficulties at the beginning of this process and toward the ultimate shift to a more equal relationship. This chapter is designed specifically for the significant other, though.

In any relationship it is unreasonable to expect that your partner will satisfy every one of your needs. We decide which of our needs we most want our partner to meet and which can be met by others. For example, it is important to me that Mike listen to me when I want to discuss something with him, but I do not expect him to repeatedly rehash this topic with me as I process it over and over. I want his support, which he gives to me, but I have learned that it irritates him to talk about the same topic again and again. Because of this, I have decided that as long as he has shown support of my concern, then I can discuss that concern over and over with someone who processes situations similarly.

When we choose to commit to someone, we need to remember that even in the most ideal of circumstances, that partner will not meet every one of our needs. We determine which are the most important for our partner to meet, and we get the others met elsewhere.

During med school, you will need to take this one step further. Like in other relationships, you will first establish your general expectations of your partner. You will engage in the process described above and learn what you require specifically from your partner and what can come from your other relationships.

You will then learn what med school requires of your med student and what relationship resources your med student still possesses once he has given med school his energy. As we have discussed, at times your partner will not have enough energy and resources remaining to meet your needs to the extent that you might like or require. When this occurs, you cannot act as if those needs do not exist. This will lead to a denial of yourself, imbalances in your relationship, and resentment toward your partner. Instead, you have to turn to other people in your life to help address your needs. This occurs in all relationships, but it is amplified during the difficult periods of med school.

You will require a support system during med school. Just like with your partner, though, no one person in your support system will fulfill all of your remaining needs. Create a system comprised of multiple people because each person will meet different needs. You have to know that when you experience a particular need, you have someone in your group who can help you to address it.

I have found that an effective support system tends to include three different kinds of important connections. The categories are not mutually exclusive; a relationship can possess multiple characteristics and any combination of these characteristics. During the difficult times in med school you will likely find all three of these different supports extremely helpful. You will need supports that are activity-based, compassion-based, and empathy-based.

Activity-based

Activity-based supports are the people with whom you can do things. These may be friends, family members, colleagues from work, teammates, participants in a hobby group, etc. You may have deep relational connections with these people or they may be casual acquaintances. In this group, the depth of your connection does not matter. The people in this group do not necessarily provide you with emotional closeness, though as I said, some may do this as well. The people in this group are companions with whom you can engage in activities.

You need people who will hang out with you on Friday night when you just want to go out and feel normal. You need people who will go to the movies, take a hike, or run errands with you. You need people to do things with!

Of course you can do these things alone, and at times you will need or even want to do them alone. However, if you do not have people to do things with during med school, you will spend a lot of time alone. Absolutely take advantage of your alone time, but also engage with people. You need to have fun.

Decide which things you want to do only with your med student. Maybe your med student really wants to do a particular activity or go to a certain place with you, or perhaps you really only want to do that activity or go to that place specifically with him. Protect the boundaries regarding what you and your partner want to do with one another. Save those items and do them together.

Anything that you are not saving to do with your partner, do with someone else. You need to live your life. If you wait for your med student, you will never do it. Interact, laugh, and engage with other people. Use the activity-based relations in your support system to keep you living and experiencing.

Compassion-based

Compassion-based supports are not in med school impacted relationships themselves, but they try to see and believe your reality for what it is. This group of people can involve friends, family, or other skilled listeners in your life. You will likely have a deeper connection with the people in this group since their role involves more emotional experiences.

Compassion-based supports know that your life and your relationship are not typical, and they will hear about it, believe you, and accept it. They do not make judgments about you or your med student. As we have discussed, your relationship does not always look healthy to an outside observer looking in, but the people in this group try to grasp the reality of the situation and the dynamics that occur. Even if they have a hard time understanding the specifics of the circumstances, they trust you, and this enables them to believe that you and your relationship are operating at your highest and healthiest capacity for this moment in time.

Compassion-based supports have an important role and satisfy an important need. They can truly talk with and listen to you. As time goes on, even though they have not lived through these circumstances themselves, they can start to develop a more complete understanding of your life and experiences. Through your descriptions, they hear so much of what transpires, and their feedback can evolve from accepting and non-judgmental to knowing and useful.

I have learned that not everyone has the capability or capacity to be a compassion-based support. I have encountered people who just do not fully grasp what I describe our experiences to be, and time has not changed this. For whatever reason, whether it be their stage of life, their limited perspective, their disconnect from our real lives, or something else entirely, these people continue to believe that med school is no harder than undergraduate studies, that I overreact, or that Mike does not make enough of an effort. They continue to believe that we lead a fairly typical existence.

It can become hard to maintain these relationships because you may feel that they do not know or understood you at this point in your life. Some of these relationships will fade. Others will appear unchanged on the surface but will feel different to you. Some will end, some will repair over time, and some will evolve if your med student's obligations start to impact that relationship. I have found a perspective shift in some people when Mike's busy, and at times unpredictable, schedule prohibits him from attending some event with them. Once they experience firsthand the limitations of med school, it can foster positive growth in the friendship. These people may never become true compassion-based supports, but it becomes easier to invest in a relationship where you feel more accepted and believed.

Empathy-based

As a social worker we are taught to very discerningly use the words "I understand" with regard to another person's life experiences. How can anyone truly understand something they have not themselves experienced? We can imagine, we can believe, we can form a picture based on someone's descriptions, and we can even generalize from our own emotional experiences, but unless we have lived through the same thing, we can only just strive to hear what another shares.

So it is with a med school impacted relationship. The compassion-based supports in our life come close to understanding. Some come closer than others. Those who experience an indirect impact by medicine understand more than those who do not. The people who see and interact with us on a weekly basis understand more than the people who do not see us regularly. People who find themselves in similar situations created by other educational or training programs understand more than those who are not in such situations.

Regardless, though, of how close a compassion-based support comes to understanding, only those who live it will truly understand. These are the empathy-based supports. Other people in your life may understand the logistics and even the majority of the emotional reality, but there are components that only significant others in committed med school relationships will understand the way you need them to.

Just as you do not become friends with everyone who shares a particular interest with you, you will not feel connected to every significant other of a med student. You will encounter significant others with basic personality differences as well as a lack of similar experiences. Every couple has its own unique experience, and med school will impact relationships in different ways and at different times. However, when you do find a significant other in a med school relationship with whom you connect, the details of your experiences will become less important than the understanding that you can each provide to the other.

You need at least one person in your support system who is also in a med school relationship and to whom you feel truly connected. If you do not have this, you need to start meeting people in these circumstances. Reach out through organized med school events, attend informal social gatherings with your med student, or ask your med student to help you connect with significant others of friends he has met. Find someone you think you connect with, and start cultivating a friendship. You need an empathy-based support. It could be the most beneficial self-care task you complete during med school.

As you cultivate these empathy-based supports, you will start to see what makes them so invaluable. They do not require words to understand you. You can call them ten minutes before a scheduled event and say, "We aren't coming. I'm really sorry", and be able to leave it at that. You do not need to explain to them that your med student is tired and cranky, had a bad day at the hospital, and now wants to bow out of the engagement without losing face or having excessive guilt. They do not need explanations, or they will accept your explanation later when you have more of an opportunity to provide it.

Your empathy-based supports are generally the only people, with the possible exception of your most closely connected compassion-based supports, around whom you do not feel silly or embarrassed when you show up alone to a dinner, a party, a wedding, or any other event where your med student was expected as well. They understand. They know he is not with you because of med school and not because he does not want to be, because he does not value you, or because your relationship is unhealthy.

It is one thing to sit at home by yourself and wish your partner had time to spend with you. It is another thing entirely to show up at an event by yourself when social custom dictates your significant other should be with you. The compassion-based supports in your life will not judge this, and they will try to make you feel as comfortable as possible. Largely, you will find a way to feel mostly comfortable with them. However, only the people who live with med school themselves can provide you with the relief of not having to explain. With them, you will likely find it possible to be completely and totally comfortable within these otherwise uncomfortable circumstances.

With empathy-based supports, you will not feel compelled to justify your relationship on any level. Because of this, you will likely vent to these people the most. They know exactly how hopeless, cold, and despondent your thoughts can become at times. You can vilify your med student to them because you know that they understand everything that remains unsaid. I do not have to qualify my emotional rant with, "Now, you know I love my husband, you know I am committed to making our relationship work, I have every ounce of sympathy and admiration for the extraordinary amount of work he puts into his day-to-day life, and I just don't know how he keeps going at times, BUT...". All of that is non-verbally understood and assumed because of shared experiences. An empathy-based support also possesses all of those wonderful feelings toward her med student, and she too has moments when she could just scream at him. We do not have to convince one another of the strength of our relationship's foundation before we just say what we feel in that instant. It is simply known and understood.

These people are invaluable, and in my life, my empathy-based supports and I have come to rely very heavily upon one another. I have activity-based supports, and I have compassion-based supports, but my empathy-based supports are irreplaceable.

You need relationships from all of the categories described here. Without a doubt, you need people who understand your circumstances and people to talk to about all that transpires in your life. However, you also need to take a break from medicine and med school. You need to go out, have fun, and think and talk about other things. You need people in your support system who promote that.

Over time, my empathy-based supports and I made other, non-med school impacted friends who we brought together into a group. This was so healthy! We still talked about med school when we needed to, but we also had a place where it became easier to remember everything else we like to do and all the other aspects of ourselves that we value and enjoy. These non-med school related friends became some of my closest compassion-based supports, and they also provided me with an opportunity to shed med school and remember everything else I bring to a friendship as well.

I would advise that you have several people in your support system with whom you feel comfortable talking. If you are anything like me and you like to talk about and process what happens in your life, you will need multiple people to serve this role. At times you will likely have a great deal to talk about, and it can become a bit of a burden to put entirely onto one other person. Sometimes even the most well intentioned of listeners can only hear so much. I also recommend that if you do not have this kind or amount of support at your disposal, consider the possibility of seeing a mental health professional, at least for a little while, simply so you have a place to verbalize, process, and work through all that you experience.

In the end, as the significant other of a med student, you have to get your needs met, and you have to do it more creatively than other people in more typical relationships. Your activity-based supports will fulfill your need for interaction, laughter, and joint activity. Your compassion-based supports will provide you with a place to talk and interact in a deeper way without being judged. Your empathy-based supports will give you relief when all you want is to not have to explain but be known. You will find people who fill different combinations of these roles, and you need them all. They will all provide you with something that you will inevitably miss at some point during your partner's time in med school.

10

Relationship Differences

As you know, I have based this book on my perspective from our relationship, but every relationship does not look like ours did. Most of the concepts in this book apply to a variety of relationship configurations, though some may require some adaptation. I have known people in many different kinds of med school impacted relationships, and I will discuss some of these relationship formations and their implications here. Keep in mind that many of these are not mutually exclusive, meaning a relationship can fit in more than one of these categories.

Multi-household Relationships
Some people in serious or committed relationships live in the same area but not in the same home. Members of these relationships can still see one another regularly because they live close in distance, but they need to plan their time together.

This has its pros and cons. At times people in these relationships may spend more quality time together because they make a concentrated effort to put aside their individual obligations and spend time alone as a couple.

At other times, though, people in this kind of relationship may suffer more greatly when the med student truly cannot put aside his obligations and therefore the couple cannot see one another at all. Sometimes sitting on the couch and watching TV together, even though not quite quality time, can feel better than not seeing one another at all. Couples who do not live together may sometimes find themselves missing this kind of connection.

Even though it may be more difficult to see one another at times, the significant other may find that she does not need to be as aware of or consider as fully the med student's idiosyncratic study habits, his studying induced mood, or his immediate needs. When not surrounded by the constant reminder of the med student's state, it can be easier to take care of oneself and not feel constantly accountable to someone who cannot always reciprocate. This can also help limit resentment, which in turn can help foster a sense of connection and investment in the relationship.

Similarly, a med student may feel relieved to know that his fluctuating mood, long hours, and intense habits may not have the same direct impact on his significant other that they might if they occupied the same home.

Long Distance Relationships

In a long distance relationship, members do not live in the same area and must travel to see one another. This involves pros and cons similar to those found in a multi-household relationship. The time that the couple spends together will more likely be quality time since they purposefully spend this time away from medicine. The significant other does not need to manage many of the day-to-day medicine related issues such as study habits, moods, and immediate needs. It can also become easier to wait to have important conversations because conversation generally requires more planning anyway.

On the other hand, it can be very difficult to find time to see one another, and couples cannot have fleeting moments of close physical proximity. Communicating regularly can also prove difficult. At times Mike and I would have less than fifteen minutes of conversation a night, and we lived in the same house. The long distance couples I know work hard to maintain some kind of regular communication and have had to compromise a great deal on both sides to make this work.

Depending on your initial expectations of a relationship, this kind of relationship can require a great deal of adjusting and accommodating. Not only does the time consuming nature of med school interfere with the relationship, the distance also does. Both partners still have schedules of their own that they need to manage, so couples have to consider several different factors when planning communication and time together. Couples in this situation may not see each other more than once a semester, and they may only talk a couple times a week. Clearly each relationship is unique and different couples will require different amounts of contact, but both partners in these relationships will likely need to negotiate major adjustments and accommodations in order for the relationship to work.

Dual Student Relationships

In some relationships, one member is a med student and another is a student, but not of med school. It can be very positive to have both members of the relationship involved in some kind of schooling or training. Because the significant other also has her own responsibilities to class, school work, and possibly employment as well, she will have less time to think about the relationship or to feel lonely. Further, when the significant other pursues her own interests and skills it can become easier to accept the time and effort that the med student invests in developing his own interests and skills.

On the other hand, these couples may find that instead of engaging in one or two-sided emotion work, no emotion work actually occurs. It can become easy to invest completely in one's own obligations and leave the relationship unattended. Because of each partners' more self oriented focus during this time, the experience of having and meeting relationship needs could diminish. This could help the relationship to thrive or it could cause it to dissipate. Again, the level of commitment by each partner to the relationship matters a great deal in these circumstances.

Additionally, couples in this situation need to ensure that both partners receive respect and accommodation while going through their schooling. At times, some med students develop the conception that their program is more difficult and thus more important than their significant others'. Med school is certainly hard, and at times it is without a doubt harder than other academic programs. At other times, though, it is not. In these relationships, both members try to balance school work, a relationship, and a life, possibly with employment as well, and both partners have the stress of having to take tests, write papers, receive grades, and do well in their programs. The strengths and ability levels of each partner further impact the stress and workload of each, as well as the consideration that each needs to give the other.

Dual Med Student Relationships

Some relationships are between med students and these bring yet another unique set of considerations. Med students in relationships with one another can have an immediate and intuitive understanding of what the other goes through. They understand time commitments, the consuming nature of what they do, and the necessity of studying so intensely. Much can go unexplained because the other has also lived through the same circumstances and thus understands.

However, obstacles can also arise. First, med students all have different strengths, habits, and methods. It can become difficult for someone who studies and takes tests with a natural ability to watch her partner struggle with the same material and schedule. It can become frustrating to feel as though you can manage your own load and see your partner unable to do the same. Similarly, it can feel disheartening to know that your partner is able to keep up and manage the workload with apparent ease while you struggle to complete your requirements for the day. In addition to creating potentially troublesome feelings between partners, these differences can also impact the already limited amount of quality time that the couple can spend together. The relationship may then suffer from lack of nurturing.

Second, obstacles can exist when med students of different years are in a relationship together. A med student in third or fourth year has a different schedule than one in first or second year, and a more seasoned med student may have a healthier balance between work and the rest of his life. It can become frustrating when one partner has the free time or is willing to make the free time for his significant other only to find she still struggles with having enough time to study for her upcoming exam.

Third, planning for residency can produce additional obstacles. This can occur in a relationship with both med students in the same class as well as between med students of different years. In the first case, both partners will look into programs simultaneously, and in the second case, one partner will start residency before the other.

If partners looking for residency placements simultaneously know that they would like to match in the same location, the matching system permits them to engage in a couples match as long as they follow the proper channels for making this request. This provides them with additional options and a higher likelihood of matching at the same institution, or at the very least in the same region.

However, some couples applying at the same time may wonder how to consider the other in this process. Do they want to engage in the couples match? Will each partner apply where he wants separately and figure out the relationship later? Will they rank programs highly in the same city and try to end up close to one another? What if one person has a dream residency placement and the other does not?

People in relationships who apply at different times may wonder the same things, though in these cases the first person to go has to decide how he will consider the other in this decision. Will he try to stay close to the one finishing med school? Will he relocate and let the other partner decide if she will follow?

It can be very difficult for a relationship to grow when both members of the relationship, whether med students, residents, or one of each, are in different locations. In these cases, both members of the relationship not only have to deal with the requirements of medicine, which in and of itself can leave little quality time together, but they also have to address the distance and conflicting schedules. These relationships can require a great deal of effort and commitment in order to continue growing.

New Relationships

I have spoken in this book about serious or committed relationships, but not all relationships fit that description. Some relationships start new just as med school begins or at some point during the course of med school. If the goal of these relationships is simply to date and have fun, then you will manage them as such. However, if you want to explore the possibility of more long-term compatibility, then you will need to consider much of what I have written in this book and apply it from the start.

Think about your expectations of a relationship and acknowledge that a new relationship with a med student will likely not meet all of these expectations. This does not mean that the relationship is not worth pursuing; it just means that you will likely need to alter your expectations a bit. The extent to which this adjustment needs to occur will also depend on when you meet your med student. If he is just starting med school, then you are about to embark on a difficult journey of transition with him, and you will need to make adjustments accordingly. If he is in his third or fourth year, you may find him a bit more settled and with a bit more free time to devote to you, and this relationship may more closely resemble what you initially had in mind.

When considering the possibility of dating someone in med school, some may decide it is not worth the effort and investment. It may not be for some. If you think you have found someone you truly want to be with, though, prepare yourself. It is 100% possible, but you will likely need at least some of the tools and perspectives outlined in this book to make it work. Change your expectations. Be prepared to manage your relationship alone at times. Find people in similar situations that can provide you with support. Always remember that if you want your relationship to work you need to keep talking, enjoy one another as often as you can, and over time re-equalize your relationship. It gets better over time, as long as you both decide you want it to work in the end.

Part Four
Establishing a New Way

11
The Shift

In the previous sections, we explored the different phases that generally occur in a med school relationship. Part Two discussed the emotional realities that frequently arise during the stressful and overwhelming times of med school, both within the relationship as a whole as well as within the significant other and med student as individuals. We also looked at the changing feeling rules and one-sided emotion work that tend to occur during this time. As we have discussed, this phase will last for different amounts of time for different couples, ranging from weeks to years.

At some point during this process, though, you will start to consider and use some of the ideas provided in Part Three. These concepts, perspectives, tools, and strategies are designed to start moving your relationship from the overwhelming phase toward a more equal and maintainable balance. The work discussed in Part Three prepares your relationship to make the ultimate shift to a more sustainable dynamic. Couples will make progress with this work at different rates. However, as you make progress in these different areas and your med student moves past his most stressful and overwhelming times, you will have the opportunity to establish your relationship in a renewed way.

I am calling the establishment of a new, healthier, sustainable dynamic in your relationship 'the shift'. When you have worked on establishing your priorities, making compromises, developing communication, expressing love, and managing your relationship's resources, you will find your relationship moving, despite med school and circumstances, into the strong, two-sided relationship you want to have.

Again, this happens at different times for different couples, and it will likely happen only once your med student starts to move away from the periods of med school overwhelm. The shift occurs partially because of a change in circumstances and partially because of growth in your relationship. You will recognize this shift, though, when you and your partner find a way to give med school fewer resources and less relationship energy and give yourselves more of it. You will see the emergence of more typical feelings rules and two-sided emotion work. Med school will always come first at times, but after your relationship experiences this shift, it becomes much easier to occasionally put med school first without it causing the devastation and angst it did in the beginning. Med school will no longer feel as if it determines the entirety of your life.

After you have engaged in the work described in the previous sections and your relationship has progressed to the point of the shift described here, it also becomes much easier to recognize if and when your relationship experiences a time of instability. Relationships have ebbs and flows, times of stability and equilibrium, and times of imbalance and disequilibrium. However, once your relationship has reached this newly defined place, you have the tools to adapt and get through the difficult times and then re-establish the new and healthy balance as these times pass.

Emotion Work

The re-emergence of the more typical two-sided emotion work is by far the most exciting change that you will see during this time period. Your feeling rules will start to more closely resemble those in other relationships again. Med student, you can start doing more for yourself. You will gain the ability to more consistently attend to topics beyond your studies and medicine, and you can have more dynamic conversations. Significant other, you will receive more support when you have a bad day, your relationship needs will be met more equally, and you can ask for favors and reasonably expect that they get done. You can once again expect your med student to make plans, do chores, and listen without getting distracted. Significant other, you will be able to stop taking care of yourself by yourself.

Doesn't this sound wonderful!? It is wonderful! However, it does not happen over night, and it does not happen without your intervention. Just as you had to take an active role in implementing the strategies from the previous section, this shift will also require your purposeful action.

Why would this need to happen so intentionally? There are two reasons. First, when you deliberately try to attain this shift, it will happen much more quickly and with your specific desired result. You can try to see what happens if you leave the process untouched, but without communication and shared goals, the chances of you and your partner ending up in a mutually desired position are extremely slim.

The second reason has to do with the fact that you and your partner may have a different level of awareness about exactly what has changed and been compromised in your relationship. As we have discussed, until you reach this point in the process, your med student will likely have been busy, preoccupied with medicine, and still experiencing support from the relationship. The significant other will likely have noticed the inequalities, the one-sided nature of the relationship, and the lack of support. Because the med student generally makes less of a relationship sacrifice than the significant other does, some med students may be truly unaware of what the significant other has managed all along. They may also have become very accustomed to the new one-sided status quo; their relationship needs are met without having to put a great deal of effort back into the relationship. Because of your different relationship positions up to this point in the process, you will need to make your shift intentional.

Mike and I always expected that his move into rotations and clinical work would foster a change in our relationship, and it did. Many couples find this a natural shifting point. Med students no longer need to study as intensely as they did during the first two years, and they start doing more hands on work, which can often feel more interesting and rewarding. However, some couples find the years of coursework easier on their relationship than those of rotations since rotations require more time at the hospital. In the end, your specific circumstances, the dynamics of your relationship, and your stress levels will determine which of these periods better compliments your relationship. For us, the elimination of the constant studying during coursework and the presence of enjoyment and excitement during clinical work helped our relationship a great deal.

When med school was stressful and overwhelming during the first couple years, we shifted our relationship into one-sided emotion work (though we did this unknowingly at the time), and as coursework progressed, we worked through the different tools and ideas presented in Part Three. We operated throughout coursework with the understanding that our relationship was a priority just as much as med school, though our relationship would need to bend and be flexible when med school could not. By the time Mike started rotations, his stress level had decreased significantly, and we had prepared our relationship through the strategies we have already discussed. Going into rotations, our relationship was ready to go through the shift and transition to a more equal state.

In our relationship, Mike had always been aware and appreciated that I did a great deal to make his life easier during the difficult times. This meant that we started the process of moving toward the shift with at least some agreement about the imbalance that had existed. However, I also knew that I had compromised even more than Mike was initially aware.

Because of this, I had to purposefully re-introduce certain balances back into our relationship.

First and foremost, you and your partner need to discuss the changes that you would both like to see occur within your relationship. Simply acknowledging the difficult emotional reality is insufficient. You also need to clearly describe the differences you would each like to see and start making plans about how to achieve this vision. We started the process of our ultimate shift with this exact conversation. We agreed that with Mike's lower stress level and increased free time, we wanted to realize certain specific changes within our relationship.

After we agreed upon these goals, we then started taking steps toward achieving our new balance. This involved re-introducing to Mike the tasks that he would once again manage. I first found myself asking for small favors. These were often just random or silly things, like getting a glass of water. When Mike was overwhelmed, I had simply done these tasks on my own in order to avoid creating more work for Mike. Once we started working toward the shift, I more readily asked him for these favors again. I also found myself stepping in less frequently to help with his chores in the house. In the past, if Mike had been extra stressed or busy, I might have helped with those things. Once he stopped experiencing that level of overwhelm, I no longer took on those tasks.

I found myself talking to Mike more, telling him more about my day and my routines. I expected the conversations to more reliably involve both of us, and I expected undivided attention and listening. As this led to more rewarding and positive interactions, I found myself being more open about what I needed and wanted in a specific moment. I would talk in detail about my bad days and expect Mike to listen and support me through the entire conversation. When I was stressed or emotionally drained, I would voice my lack of interest or ability to listen to and support him completely.

At times Mike expressed some confusion about why I would now ask all this of him. He was not unwilling to do these things; it had simply not been our norm for so long. When he expressed confusion, I pointed out that for multiple years I had managed all of this on my own, and now our relationship and circumstances had progressed to a place where I no longer had to do it all on my own. He understood and responded accordingly.

I am not sure that a med student can ever completely understand the relationship position of the significant other because it is so fundamentally different from the relationship position of the med student (just as a significant other cannot completely understand the work load and job of a med student). However, as you engage in these steps toward two-sided emotion work and your med student starts taking responsibility again for aspects of the relationship he has not managed in quite some time, his perspective can start to shift. He will never have experienced what the significant other did, just as the significant other will never have experienced what he did. However, as he starts filling his role in the relationship again, he can begin to see just how much he was unable to do previously and therefore how much his significant other did in his place.

ιow that Mike is much more available to me, I use him as a resource in a way that I did not before. By contrasting his role in my emotional life previously to his role in my emotional life now, he has seen just how much I managed without him and did for him so that he could focus so completely on the unyielding and uncompromising task at hand. Now he sees his role in our relationship more clearly. He can see his tasks and responsibilities, and now that he has the time, energy, and brain space to do them on his own, he does them on his own.

On my side, I accept and find gratefulness in what Mike can once again do in our relationship. I do not wallow in past resentments or hold over him the times of past unavailability. This shift requires that both partners move into the present together with joy and appreciation for what your relationship can now achieve, not dwell in bitterness about any previous circumstances.

Acceptance

We have talked a great deal about acceptance in this book. We started in Part Two when we looked at the role acceptance plays in first creating one-sided emotion work, as well as in managing grief and resentment. We further explored acceptance as we discussed priorities, communication patterns, and the qualities in a successful med school relationship. While working toward two-sided emotion work is the ultimate goal within your relationship, acceptance needs to be an additional personal goal for a significant other.

When you can accept your choices, your feelings, and the realities and constraints of med school, you will find peace and freedom where you may not have thought it possible. When you take ownership for your own personal experience, you will be more forgiving and less inclined to foster guilt in your partner. When you can be supportive of, listen to, and brainstorm with your partner but then relinquish his emotional experiences to him and not take them on yourself, you will find it easier to cultivate calm in your daily life. When you decide that you no longer want to complain about your reality but instead find a way to make it into a worthwhile life, you will start to appreciate the joy you already experience and value the life you already have.

When you have reached a state of acceptance regarding all of this, you will find it easier to do everything I have outlined in this book. It becomes easier to remain present focused and not catastrophize, to seek out and cultivate other relationships, to invest in yourself and your own growth, to see a future and get excited about it, and to want your relationship to thrive.

Acceptance is a process. It evolves over time and through different areas of your life. At least some acceptance is necessary in order to create the circumstances required for the shift to occur. However, acceptance also seems to come with more ease, sincerity, and depth once the shift has transpired within your relationship.

The increase of acceptance after the shift may happen because your relationship more closely resembles a typical relationship again. It may occur because you now believe that you will make it through this journey together. Perhaps you know that even though more obstacles and difficult times will come, you and your partner have reached a better place in your relationship and have more faith in your abilities moving forward. For whatever reason, acceptance seems to come more readily once you reach this point in your journey.

Until you get through the shift, the process of maintaining a relationship in med school can take a great deal of effort. Very little about it feels intuitive, particularly when you first start out. We like to think that relationships should unfold naturally and without so much intervention. The reality is, though, that this does not happen even in non-med school relationships. Relationships take work. Sometimes they take more work than at other times. In med school, they take a lot of work. Once you reach this shift, though, they will not always require as much as they did previously.

The shift is an exciting time. Let it be exciting! You have worked very hard to get to this point, and you, as individuals and as a couple, deserve to feel good about this accomplishment! There is something empowering about reclaiming the balance in your relationship.

As your journey through medicine continues, you will have to adapt and resort to less than appealing roles at times, but once this shift occurs, your relationship has asserted its new capability. From this point forward, any deviation can be more short-term because neither you nor your partner will want to tolerate the former one-sided way for very long.

You cannot undo all the work you put in to get to this new point. You cannot forget what this new balance feels like. In the future when medicine needs to temporarily take over, you can now know that your relationship has the capability to right itself again once the stressful times pass.

Troubleshooting

If you find yourself, your partner, or your relationship struggling in such a way that you question the possibility of this shift occurring, consider some of the following thoughts.

First, please know that this does not mean that there is something 'wrong' with you, your partner, or your relationship. It can mean many things, but there is no element of 'wrong'.

It could simply mean that your process through these steps has taken longer than you had thought it would. There is no specific time frame for reaching the shift, and it could be that one or all of your stages along the way have taken longer than you anticipated.

It could also mean that your process through med school has been fundamentally different from the one I have presented here. You may simply not see any real similarities between the experiences I present and the reality that you have lived. This is completely fine! Your path has just been different!

If you notice resistance on the part of your med student, he could have uncertainty about organizing his priorities. Have a discussion about how he values the different components of his life and how he hopes to connect his values with his actions. Refer back to Chapter 7 for more on this topic.

Your med student may also have a difficult time relinquishing one-sided emotion work. Some med students come to enjoy one-sided emotion work since it involves little effort for a big return. If you believe that this is happening in your relationship, then significant other, you may need to explain in more detail your experience of one-sided emotion work. Refer back to Part Two for help explaining these ideas to your partner. You may also find it helpful to re-explore and redefine together your priorities and goals as a couple. This may help your med student to remember the importance of your joint commitment and investment. If your med student still struggles to understand, you may find it useful to pursue couples therapy. I present information regarding this at the end of the chapter.

Additionally, your med student may still feel extremely stressed and overwhelmed. If this is the case, then it may take some more time before the shift can occur. Work on introducing small steps toward your ultimate goal. This can help you to feel you are making progress while your med student does not experience the stress of too many new responsibilities all at once. Chapter 7 specifically and Part Three as a whole outline some small steps that you can make over time.

If you notice resistance within yourself, significant other, you may have some difficulty with the idea of acceptance. It can be hard to accept the realities and difficulties of med school. It can be even harder to acknowledge that your own choices have had a role in creating your current circumstances. It can also be difficult to take ownership for managing your own feelings, particularly when your partner is available to blame for them. Remember, though, that you are responsible for your feelings and circumstances just as much as your partner is responsible for his. The theme of acceptance is located throughout this book, so refer back to these areas, particularly Part Two, Chapter 6 and this chapter. Acceptance does take time to develop, but ultimately it is your responsibility to reach this state, and only you can get yourself there. If you continue to operate without any acceptance, you essentially take on the role of martyr and decide that you have fallen victim to your own life. And this is simply not true.

You may also find it difficult to reach the shift if you did not make accommodations for your relationship in the first place. You may have gone through med school without making any changes to feeling rules and emotion work. If this is the case, you have nothing to shift back from. Even still, you may find yourself dissatisfied with the current state of your relationship and want to improve it in some way. Refer back to Part Three as well as this chapter and see if you can start implementing some of the strategies that encourage a move toward a healthier relationship.

Additionally, you could find attaining the shift problematic if you do not actually want your relationship to last. Being in a relationship that involves medicine is hard; there is no doubt about it. It is normal to question if your relationship is worth all this work. If you decide that it is not worth the work, then your relationship will not successfully pass through the shift. This is your decision and only you and your partner know what you are willing and able to handle together.

If you, your partner, or both of you together are struggling in a way from which you do not know how to recover, and you want your relationship to work, seek professional counsel. There are counselors and therapists from the fields of social work, counseling, marital and family therapy, and psychology (among others depending on the state in which you live) who do individual and couples therapy. Ask people you trust for the names of skilled providers in your community. Your primary care doctors may be able to make referrals. Look at your insurance plans for providers. Ultimately, your provider should make you feel safe, heard, and not judged. You should be involved in the direction of your treatment, and if you find that you are not, seek another provider. Having a neutral and capable support system can be invaluable at a time like this.

12

The Silver Lining:
Learning Strategic Self-Care

We have explored in detail the emotional path that you and your relationship may traverse during med school, from the difficult times of overwhelm, through the work phase, and to the ultimate shift to a more preferred state. I have emphasized repeatedly that while you will cultivate change in your relationship and work toward a healthier and more equal state, you will not be able to change the circumstances of med school. You will need to accept this reality and work within it.

Reaching the shift does not only benefit your relationship. On a more personal level, reaching this point in the process enables your own perspective to broaden. Where you once saw difficulties, obstacles, and limits, now you can see opportunities, chances, and options. What initially felt problematic can actually become appreciated and useful.

In this chapter, I will present ways that significant others have discovered that they can use the realities of med school to their advantage and for the benefit of their own self-care. This list is far from inclusive, and many tools, strategies, and self-care hints throughout the book are not listed in this section. Instead, consider this a compilation of self-care tips derived directly from the very difficulties that med school can present.

Pursue your dreams. Have your own goals, plans, and vision for your career, family, and growth as a person. Yes, some of these need to coincide with your med student, but some of them are truly your own. Pursue your own growth and development while your med student pursues his. This is the perfect time to take your own classes, work toward a promotion, gain a new skill, achieve a personal goal, or devote your time to something important to you. Your med student will be busy pursuing his dreams; there is no reason you cannot pursue yours as well!

Do something you like. Make sure that you are happy doing whatever occupies much of your time, whether your job, your schooling, or raising your family. It is okay to have bad days, and you do not always have to be happy. You and your med student can even be unhappy at the same time. However, if you both find yourselves stuck in a fairly permanent state of misery, your relationship will suffer. Enjoy what you spend the bulk of your day doing.

Leave the house. You will need a change of scenery whether or not your med student studies at home. If he does study at home, though, you will definitely need to leave the house at times, particularly before exams. This can be a miserable time for a med student, and he will likely feel stressed, tired, and cranky. It is hard to be in a house with that atmosphere and not feel hopeless yourself, so make plans for those times and leave the house for a while if possible.

Reward yourself. You work harder in this relationship than anyone will ever know. Treat yourself well for all your hard work. Go to the spa, take a hike, go for a drive, buy a new pair of shoes, go visit a friend, spend the day at the beach, leave the house, light candles, buy your favorite dessert, do take out- whatever! Pamper yourself. Make other areas of your life easier when you can. You have earned it!

Explore. Med school can bring people to new locations, and you may find yourself living in a place you do not intend to stay forever. Even if you plan to live in that location for the rest of your life, though, explore your town, state, and region of the country. Take afternoon trips, day trips, and weekend trips. Learn the local attractions. Have fun with it! You can find things to do no matter where you are, so go do them, especially if you may not ever return to the area again. Take advantage while you can!

Learn to love on call time. At the beginning of clinical work, it can feel like an intrusion to have your med student on call. Shift your perspective. Instead of feeling as though you have lost time with your med student, see this for the good it brings. You have time to do whatever you want! Have friends over, go out to dinner, watch a favorite movie, dance around the house, or do nothing! You should do whatever you want to do or whatever you cannot do when your med student is around.

You have a break from being responsible and accountable for this period of time, so use it to recharge yourself. If you became accustomed to having time alone when your partner studied all the time, you may find the presence of on call time refreshing! Enjoy it!

You cannot do it for your med student. You are not responsible for your med student's moods or for completing his tasks. You can support him, listen when he needs to talk, and brainstorm when he needs help problem solving. You cannot do it for him, though. You can be there for your med student, but once he returns to his studies or to the hospital, you need to know how to escape the overwhelm and depression that will accompany him at times. If you do not learn how to do this, you will start to experience these feelings yourself, and then you will encounter difficulties not only when supporting him but when managing your own stresses as well.

Do not let the past or the future become toxic to the present. You will reach a point in med school where your present situation feels significantly better than the months and years leading up to it. Do not ruin this time by constantly thinking about and comparing it to the past. Enjoy your present moment, especially if it feels better than past moments! Likewise, thinking about, worrying about, and anticipating the future can also damage the present. Yes, the future requires thought, and yes, planning is necessary. Make your plans, though; do not obsess about them. It is okay, and even healthy, to experience a little dose of denial with regard to all that is still unsettled in the future in order to help you better enjoy the present. You have earned your positive present reality, so make the most of it!

Part Five
Moving Forward

13
Future Planning

As med school comes to an end, you will find yourselves looking to the future. As with so many other aspects of med school, when planning for and moving toward the future, you will have several different logistical and emotional realities to consider. Emotionally, we think about our relationship, our internal processes, and our hopes for the future. Logistically, we think about issues of time, money, and location.

Completing med school and moving to the next step is exciting, but the next step can still feel daunting. At this time, many significant others of med students think about their hopes for the future and find themselves asking the question, "How is my partner's career going to affect the rest of my life?"

We discussed in Chapter 4 the possibility of experiencing a grief reaction regarding the changes that med school can cause in the vision you had for your life. In Chapter 5 we talked about the resentment that can emerge while going through this process and how this can impact your vision of your partner and of your relationship. We talked about the necessity of experiencing these different emotions, as well as ultimately finding a state of acceptance regarding your new reality.

As significant others start looking toward the future and asking the question, "How is medicine going to impact the next stages of my life?", feelings of loss and resentment can re-emerge. You know that med school has already impacted so much, and you cannot help but wonder how the medical institution will continue to impact your life. Med students may have similar questions of their own and wonder about the impact that their commitment to medicine will have on the rest of their life as well.

You both may start to ponder your med student's upcoming responsibilities and time commitments and then contrast them with what you had envisioned for this next stage of your life. For many couples, this next stage of life involves topics such as living together, marriage, children and families, moves, purchasing homes, and finances. At this point, you hopefully have new expectations for your relationship after having progressed to a more stable and sustainable place over the years of med school. Even still, though, it makes sense to wonder how medicine will continue to impact your life.

In reality, your vision for your future and medicine's options for your future do not always match. At times they connect, and that is very fortunate, but at times they do not. Further, a med student and a significant other will sometimes have different visions for the future and disagree about the extent to which medicine should be factored into future related decisions.

I am going to introduce a concept here that can help us to discuss the future and address the feelings of powerlessness that can occur during this stage of your relationship and the medical process.

Locus of Control

Locus of control is a concept used in mental health to describe the source of power or control that an individual perceives as dictating the course of his life. Possessing an internal locus of control means that an individual perceives himself as being in control of or responsible for an outcome. Having an external locus of control means a person perceives something outside of himself as responsible for an outcome (Rotter, 1954).

This occurs on a spectrum. In the middle is a confident, mentally healthy human being. This person generally perceives a slightly more internal locus of control for positive outcomes and a slightly more external locus of control for negative outcomes. This comes with an understanding, though, that sometimes outcomes, both positive and negative, happen because of our own actions and at other times they happen because of outside forces. More self centered or arrogant individuals occupy one end of the spectrum, and they tend to see positive outcomes as completely internally created and negative outcomes as completely due to external forces. Individuals who have low self-esteem or who are depressed occupy the other end, and they tend to see negative outcomes as internally created and positive outcomes as externally created.

In mental health, we look at internal and external locus of control as they relate to positive and negative outcomes. In med school, though, I have noticed that I look at internal and external locus of control as they relate to the size of the outcome. It can often feel as though we have control over the small things that occur in our lives, but the larger issues can feel externally controlled and driven. For example, I may control what we have for dinner tonight, but I do not control where we will move for residency.

Over time, as people perceive a constant inability to impact their own existence, or when they see aspects of their lives as externally controlled, they can develop what is called learned helplessness (Ashford, LeCroy, & Lortie, 2006). When this occurs, a person does not believe that he has the ability or power to influence a set of circumstances. He feels 'helpless' to make an impact because he has 'learned' through past experiences that he cannot. At times during the medicine process it can feel as though we do not have the ability to impact the way our lives unfold. It can feel as though we are helpless and unable to influence the system. However, this is only partially true.

I am going to explore several different components of planning for the future. I will look at how they relate to med school and medicine, as well as to locus of control and learned helplessness. I will also address both the logistical and emotional elements of each as well.

Residency and Fellowships

For many med school relationships, planning for residency is the first post-med school step that occurs. Your med student's ultimate residency placement will impact both of your lives in a variety of ways. Because of this, you will both need to think about the components of a residency program that you find the most important before your med student engages in the match process and starts applying to programs as discussed in Chapter 1.

First and foremost, your med student needs to choose a specialty to pursue. It seems intuitive that a med student would choose the specialty he is most interested in, and largely this makes sense. However, specialties can differ significantly with regard to their competitiveness, locations of programs, number of positions available, length of the program, and hours worked during the program. This means that your med student may have limited options based on his competitiveness as an applicant, your preferences on where to live, and the time commitment he is willing to make to his residency.

Further, each specialty offers a different kind of lifestyle after residency and will vary based on job opportunities, salaries, hours worked, on-call schedules, and malpractice considerations. People find some branches of medicine more conducive than others to having a relationship and family. This does not mean you cannot have a relationship or family in a more competitive or time-consuming specialty, but it does mean a significant other will need to make concessions, and a med student will have to work much harder at maintaining a balanced life.

Med students and significant others may both find themselves with mixed feelings as they weigh the pros and cons of different specialty options. A med student may consider his love for a particular specialty, the length of a residency program, the relocation options, and his chances of matching into that specialty. A significant other may find herself considering how each specialty impacts the availability of her partner, the time commitment her partner will need to make, and the length of time the program will last.

At this point in time, some significant others have felt tempted to ask their med student to consider choosing a less competitive or less time-consuming specialty in order to limit further stress on the relationship. If a med student truly has no preference between two specialties, then this may be a legitimate request.

However, if a med student has a clear first choice specialty and his significant other still asks him to choose another, that med student risks entering into an unfulfilling career path and then developing a great deal of resentment toward his partner and their relationship. Many med students enter into competitive and time-consuming specialties and still have families and successful relationships. Many couples opt to pursue a first choice specialty and find ways to manage their relationships within this context so that they do not later look back with regret and what-ifs.

After choosing a specialty, you will both then think about the other components of a residency program that you value. You may consider the quality and location of a program, the proximity of friends and family, or the presence of a certain type of living. You may be interested in future opportunities such as research or fellowships, or you may want a specific balance between work, family, and leisure.

Once you both have decided on the important aspects of a program, your med student will know more clearly where to apply. He will submit his applications and then receive interviews. After completing the interviews, he will rank his selections based on your joint list of important criteria. He will then submit this ranked list into the matching system.

As a couple, you have control over the components of the residency matching process listed above. You choose a specialty, programs to apply to, and the order of your rank list. However, as individuals within that couple, you have different roles and maintain different levels of control.

Med student, you have control over your presentation as an applicant. You may engage in extra research, do away rotations at other universities, or network with useful contacts. You put together your curriculum vitae and write a personal statement for your residency application. You will eventually go on interviews and do what you can to make a positive impression. You control the places you apply, the interviews you accept, and the rank list you submit. Ideally, you will consider your partner's opinions throughout this process, but in the end, you have the ultimate control over all of these components.

Significant other, you have much less control in this situation. Your med student's residency placement impacts your life just as completely as it impacts his, and yet you can do very little to actively affect this process on your own. Essentially, any impact you make on this process needs to go through your med student first. He needs to consider your opinions in his choices because you do not have the power to make any of those choices yourself.

Med students, if you find yourself having a hard time taking your partner's opinions into consideration, spend some time reflecting on what might be getting in the way. Are you fearful of not matching and feel as though any placement is better than no placement? Are you attached to one particular 'ideal' program that has represented a dream or measure of competence along the way? Do you still have difficulty accepting that you are both in this together and that you both need to make life-altering decisions together?

At this time it becomes particularly important to understand how the choices you make regarding residency impact your partner. Residency impacts both of your lives as well as your relationship, but in the end only you get to submit a list of your preferred programs. You will both have preferences and opinions about this process, and you need to listen to your partner's perspective. You may encounter differences of opinion, but the resolutions you reach are much less important than the way you reach them. You and your partner need to talk about every aspect of this process, and you need to understand that your partner can only have a say over this next stage of her life through you and your respect for her preferences.

This can be a difficult time for significant others. If you find yourself feeling uninvolved or powerless, find ways to contribute. When Mike looked into residency locations, I did too.

I spent time on the computer reading about all the different programs, looking up their locations, and developing informed opinions. Mike and I would then talk about what we each had learned through our research. Once Mike interviewed at different programs, I felt more connected to the process and had a better idea about what each interview meant for us.

If it is possible and desirable, you can travel with your med student while he goes on his interviews. No, you cannot sit in the room and make an impact the way your med student can, but you can see the different schools and areas. If you cannot travel during the interview time, maybe you can make a trip together once the interviews have ended and visit some of the different locations on your list. Many programs permit students to contact current residents with questions. You can have your med student ask some of your questions, or you can see if you can contact someone for information as well. These actions can go a long way in helping you to feel more involvement and control in this process that so directly impacts your life.

In the case of residency, neither partner in your relationship has complete control over the ultimate match, but without a doubt, the med student has much more of an opportunity to directly impact this process. The significant other can only make an indirect impact through the med student. Therefore, if the outcome of this process is as important to the significant other as it is to the med student, the med student needs to consider the significant other's perspective and permit her a role in this process.

Finances

While residency is a fairly universal next step for graduating med students, other future oriented plans will likely vary significantly amongst med school couples. However, at the base of most future oriented plans is the consideration of finances.

Many med students take out loans to pay for their medical schooling. They may also use loans to cover their living expenses since they do not have the time to hold a job while in med school. This can create an immense amount of debt that will impact both of your lives.

If your med student has federal and educational loans, if they remain solely in the med student's name, and if you do not consolidate them with any of the significant other's loans, then the significant other will never have responsibility for paying them back should something happen to the med student. You can, and probably should, contact your loan carrier to ensure that this is in fact the case. Also remember that private loans may operate differently.

Even though the loans technically belong to one partner, they will affect both of you as you go through your lives together. As you determine your financial plan and budget, you will need to take into account the repayment of these loans. You may realize that you require more income to meet your financial needs. Unfortunately, residents do not have the opportunity to ask for pay increases, and they cannot look for better paying jobs. Programs determine salaries even before students match, so when a student matches, he is contracted to that salary. This means that the variability and flexibility for additional income will either remain with the significant other or involve the resident seeking additional employment in accordance with program restrictions.

Fortunately, active July 1, 2009, a law was passed stating that repayment of federal loans can be based on income level if you choose this option. This can help enormously since it can change your monthly payment from a couple thousand dollars to a few hundred dollars. The law states that a person can use this plan as long as he chooses, so this can help not only during residency but also during fellowships as well. A person would not need to make a larger monthly payment until he earned a full time physician's salary.

Income based repayment can help you both to live more comfortably during residency by removing some of the pressure and financial stress that can occur with a higher monthly payment. In addition, it can also help couples to more realistically plan for things they may desire at this stage of life, such as purchasing homes and starting families. This can then increase your sense of control over these aspects of your future as well.

Moving and Homes

When looking to a buy a home, the current economic climate and the lending institution that you choose will partially determine how influential your existing debt will be in this process. At times the debt will be considered a liability, and at times it may be overlooked in favor of your med student/ resident's ultimate earning potential. Some lending institutions cater specifically to med students and residents. These operate with the awareness that graduating med students and residents do have a greater earning potential and are less likely to default on their payments. With these institutions, issues like down payments and payment plans may have more flexibility up front.

When purchasing a home, additional considerations exist that go beyond basic finances and that relate to the concept of control. During med school and residency (and possibly fellowship as well), you can only know where you will live for a few years at a time. Further, you only learn of your next location just as your current position comes to a close. This means you only have a small window of time to prepare for your next step. Some people may never actually have to move because of medicine, and others may move four or five times over the course of a decade. In either case, though, it is only upon the closing of one step that you will have certainty about the next one.

Some people find the idea of moving frequently and buying and selling homes every few years quite desirable. Others may find this unsettling. If you tend to fit the first description, then medicine can provide you with a terrific way to relocate and enjoy new areas. If you prefer to buy a home, put your time and energy into making it your own, and live there indefinitely, then the training years of medicine make this a more difficult goal to achieve.

The availability of your med student/resident also factors in when making the decision to purchase a home. Through most of med school and residency, your med student will be unable to fully commit to just about anything that would occur during business hours. If someone needs to be in your home to let in a worker, deal with a repairman, or accept a delivery, it will likely need to be the significant other. Further, med students and residents, particularly as they start their programs, will likely have little leftover time and energy for house maintenance, repairs, or upkeep. This means that at times these will fall to the significant other, require intervention by someone else, or remain unfinished until the most stressful and overwhelming times pass.

The potential for multiple moves throughout medical training raises other points unrelated to the purchasing of homes, particularly for the significant other. Each move requires starting over and re-establishing many elements of your lives. For med students/residents, this is at least partially done for you. You are moving because of your next step, so you have a guarantee that you at least have a job and a built-in set of peers.

Significant others, depending on how long you have lived in your previous location, you could very well leave an established career, a group of friends, and the life you have grown accustomed to. If you have used the tools in this book, then you have hopefully developed a fulfilling life for yourself in your current location. Starting over is not impossible, particularly since you take everything you have already learned and developed with you, but it does take effort, and as we have stated multiple times throughout this book, these changes can bring not only excitement but sadness and loss as well.

While you do not ultimately control where you go next, you can control how you handle the situation. Experience any sadness, loss, and anger that arise. If you have liked your life in your current location, decide to create an equally good life for yourself in your next location. You have done it once, so you can do it again. If you have not liked your life in your current location, use this as a time to start over and do things differently. You have the opportunity not only to replicate positive areas from your previous life, but also to make improvements in any area that you felt was lacking before. As hard as it may be to leave your current location, try to use this as a time to continue growing and expanding the positive in your life. In essence, exert control in your life in the areas where you can.

Family Planning

Deciding if and when to have children can be a very difficult decision to make when considering medicine. Not only will a couple have financial and logistical considerations when factoring in the cost of a child, loan repayment, possible purchasing of homes, and potential relocation every few years, but they will have emotional and relational considerations as well.

When a couple decides to have a child, not only in a med school relationship but in any relationship, the dynamics within that relationship will change. While it is not within the scope of this book to explore this change in detail, at its most basic level, it involves a new entity in your relationship that requires a great deal of time, energy, and resources. Members of a relationship now have to share their attention and resources between their partner and their child, so fewer resources get directed specifically at the relationship.

If your relationship has reached a point of mutuality and stability as described in Part Four, then your relationship will likely absorb this new entity and adapt with more ease and confidence. If you find that med school or medicine still feels like a third entity in your relationship and still acts as a determining factor, then your adjustment to a child joining your relationship may be more difficult or precarious. This does not mean it is not possible or that the adjustments will not occur; it means there is a difference between starting from a strongly established foundation as compared to a still unsettled and contentious point.

Even if you believe you are having a child from a strong and stable foundation, you will still need to think about matters with regard to medicine. First, you will need to decide what role you want your med student/resident to have in the lives of your children. Just as we discussed priorities for the relationship in Chapter 7, a discussion needs to occur about the priorities for your new family. Not only do you need to figure out how your children get prioritized along with your relationship and medicine, you also need to make plans about how you will actively realize those priorities in your daily life. A med student/resident will not always have a great deal of time at home with his family, so make plans about how you intend to use that time in ways that promote your priorities.

You will also need to pay attention to the amount of support each partner receives once children are present. If a med student/resident balances work and family with the support of his partner, but a significant other balances home, children, and possibly employment without the consistent support of her partner, these can feel very different. Hopefully, the imbalance in support has subsided over time as the shift in your relationship occurred, but during particularly busy times for the med student/resident this can start to polarize again. You simply need to address it in order to return to a more equal partnership.

Lastly, I would like to note that issues related to having children and starting families can unfold differently depending on the gender configuration in the relationship. When the significant other carries the child, pregnancy and parenting do not necessarily need to have a major impact on the med student/resident's career, but the impact on the significant other will likely be much higher. Due to the time commitment of medicine, she will likely have to do much more without her partner than someone in a relationship not impacted by medicine. Many couples consider this while deciding when they want to start having children.

On the other hand, when the med student/resident carries the child, pregnancy and parenting will have more of an impact on her medical career. Many female med students/residents who want to have children think about all they have invested in their dream of becoming a doctor and wonder at what point it makes sense or is feasible to introduce a pregnancy. If a female med student or resident has a child during her medical training, there is a considerable chance that her training will be postponed at least for a time. This could involve making up what she missed at an accelerated pace or pushing back a graduation/completion date. No easy answers exist in this situation, but many female med students and residents who want to have children commonly make these considerations.

Through med school I have learned that we may carefully and thoughtfully develop plans, but they rarely happen just as we envision. Many factors impact our lives, not only with regard to medicine but in all aspects of life, and we only have control over some of them. It is important to have goals and dreams and to see a general path toward their achievement. Until you move along that path, though, you cannot know what obstacles, turns, and detours will arise. When you encounter these, it does not mean that your dreams have disappeared; you simply need to take a different route to reach them. Your plan, or your path toward achievement has changed, not the actual goals and dreams. In the end, the path you take is your life. It makes you who you are, and as long as you still hold the same goals and dreams, your path can always lead you to them.

When all is said and done, we will encounter many situations along our medical paths that we cannot control as completely as we might like. External circumstances impact some situations and can leave us feeling as though we lack an internal locus of control, but we are not helpless.

First, we determine our ultimate goals and dreams and the general direction our paths will take. We may not like all the components of medicine, but we have chosen this path because we see an end in it we like. For our med students this end is a career they love. For us as significant others, it is a life with a person we love. This path may wind in ways we could have never predicted, but if we hold tight to our goals and dreams, our path will find a way there.

Second, when confronted with external circumstances from medicine that we do not like and that cause us to question our own impact, we can still determine what happens within the confines of these circumstances. We may encounter limiting factors from medicine that other people do not have to deal with, but other people have their own limiting factors that we may not have to handle. We exert our influence where we can, choose how to address an obstacle, and chart our new path around it. It can definitely feel good sometimes to be mad at medicine for setting these limits in the first place, but once you finish being mad, those limits will still exist, and you can still find ways to make your plans work and achieve happiness. As you repeatedly evoke the control you have as opposed to your sense of helplessness, you will find it becomes progressively easier to see the role you do have in directing your own life.

14
Social Change

Social workers by profession are concerned not only with what occurs on an individual, or micro, level, but also with what occurs on a larger scale, or at the macro level. This book has largely focused on the individual and his intimate, romantic relationship. I have addressed the issue of relationships in med school from the perspective of the relationship, with an emphasis on the individuals' need to adapt.

However, as a social worker, I also think about the more macro level changes that could, and arguably should, occur in order to impact positive change in an individual's relationships and personal life. Throughout our time in med school, I noticed several practices and expectations within the med school curriculum and program that actually seem to hinder a med student's education, not to mention his personal life.

My largest concern is the lack of emphasis on helping students to develop the well-rounded, balanced, and healthy lifestyle that doctors try to teach to their patients. It does not make sense that a med student finds himself in a situation where the only way to succeed involves forgoing sleep, nutrition, exercise, relaxation, leisure, and relationships. Doctors encourage their patients to cultivate these very items when lifestyle and stress impact their illnesses. Why are med students groomed to overlook all of this in their own lives?

Some say that med school is a "right of passage" and since previous generations of doctors had to deal with these grueling requirements, then current students also must struggle through. Those who come out the other side then truly 'deserve' the title Doctor.

I find this ridiculous.

With new technology, understanding, and awareness, nearly every aspect of our lives has changed and evolved over time, thus making many things different for the current generation than it was for previous generations. Sometimes things become easier, sometimes they become more complex. The reality is, though, that the present and past are different. We are expected to deal with and manage this in every other aspect of our lives, so why would or should it be any different with regard to medical training?

Many med students have reflected that tremendous medical advances have occurred in the past ten to twenty years. Med students learn all of these new advances; however, they also still learn all of the past interventions as well. This means that med students today learn the same content that a med student did twenty years ago as well as everything that has happened since then. When people say that med school today is just as hard as it was twenty years ago, that is not exactly true. Med students today learn more material in the same amount of time, and they have to know and understand all of it. This contributes to the lack of balance a med student can experience between his training and the other areas of his life.

The testing practices present in some programs can also add to this lack of balance. Some programs have students take tests one day and then start a new unit of lectures the next day. For example, when Mike first started his program, he took exams on Mondays which meant that he would study all weekend, take his test on Monday, and then start a new unit with lecture on Tuesday. This translates into no scheduled breaks or days off throughout an entire semester. Four months without even one day of reprieve. I cannot help but wonder who this could possibly benefit.

As I described earlier, a med student frequently uses any and all available time to study and stay caught up, so the chances of him taking a weekend off and not studying are close to non-existent. Many med students only take substantial breaks if they truly have nothing to do, and they only have nothing to do after finishing an exam. If exams happen on Fridays, students can then use the weekend after the exam to regroup instead of waiting for the end of the semester to do so. This is much healthier for the med student and for his relationships. Fortunately, Mike's program chose to do this part way through his training.

The issue of maintaining balance in one's life exists even beyond med school. In 2003, the Accreditation Counsel of Graduate Medical Education created new standards for resident duty hours stating that residents can no longer work more than 80 hours a week. Some programs initially struggled with this limitation, expecting their residents to work over 80 hours and then to misrepresent the hours they had worked on their time sheets. In the years following this new regulation, the dishonesty was largely addressed through reprimands and penalties for programs engaging in these behaviors. Today, many programs do try to abide by the 80 hour work week. The 80 hours include normal shift hours as well as overnight call at the hospital.

This is certainly a step in the right direction for encouraging a healthy, balanced lifestyle for residents. Working more than 80 hours a week essentially prohibits any kind of rewarding life outside of work, so this limit has definite benefits. However, 80 hours a week devoted to work is still a lot. Once again, though, the argument I have heard against any further restriction of hours is that previous generations learned quite effectively by working more than 80 hours a week, therefore it must stand to reason that decreasing the hours worked in a week would only negatively impact learning.

Yes, a resident may miss out on some learning opportunities if he is in the hospital fewer hours a week, but at least he will be awake, alert, and interested when he is there. As I see it, that may actually increase his likelihood of learning and remembering something new! In addition, I don't know about you, but I do not feel very comfortable with the idea that my doctor might be on hour 78 when he provides services, particularly skilled procedures, to me.

I understand that being a physician requires a broad knowledge base and specialized training, the scope of which does not even begin to touch that required in many other fields. I also understand that the stakes are higher because at times, health and illness can be a matter of life and death. Therefore physicians do need to be fully prepared to do their job correctly as soon as they start working independently.

I do not understand, though, the dismissal of the medical professional's life outside of medicine. Physicians are still people who have families, relationships, stressors, feelings, and needs. They have to forget about medicine sometimes. Not only does this provide balance in the rest of their life, but it also allows them to return to medicine with a clear head. If I thought about social work and my clients all the time, I would be useless to everyone. I would no longer think clearly about my responsibilities as a social worker because it would consume me. I can only go back every day and be available to my clients because I take time every day to not be available to them. I take time to just be me, enjoy my relationships, relax, and do things that make me happy. Our training as social workers emphasizes this element of self-care and self-preservation. We learn the importance of managing our own mental and physical health, not only so we become stronger and happier as individuals but also so we can bring more to our clients. I have not seen this emphasized in medical training in quite the same way, and I do not understand why.

I have seen medical training put an indirect pressure on its trainees to believe that success comes with being all consumed. This may get students through their training, but then what? They have then been exposed to a culture that encourages them to grow into physicians who lack balance and healthy lifestyles.

I think it is unfair to groom people to take care of the needs of others while making it near impossible for them to take care of their own needs. In my opinion, this is not a healthy system. Unfortunately, you are trying to develop a healthy relationship within this system.

What can we do about this system? To be honest, I am not sure. I think the majority of the change needs to come from those who are in or have gone through the system: our med students, residents, and physicians. I know some in the system fear that they will risk their own well being by challenging the status quo. Upon exiting the system, many feel tired and relieved, and they do not want to make any more effort.

I think we need to let the system know our displeasure, though. After completing a med school or residency program, I think it is important to leave feedback, whether as a student or as a significant other. I do not know what difference it could make, but it is certainly worth trying once you can be certain that leaving this feedback can no longer negatively impact the student.

In the meantime, while we try to make changes to the system, med students will need to find a way to make things work within the current system. Med students need to make a commitment to themselves and to their relationships that they will try to stay as healthy as possible. That may mean taking time off, ensuring they exercise, or not eating junk food at the hospital for lunch. It may mean doing one fun thing a week, taking a vacation, or sleeping. Until the system changes, med students need to find a way to stay healthy and to cultivate at least some of the balance and healthy lifestyle that they will preach to their patients some day.

Significant other, you need to help them make sure this happens. Your presence alone, even if not as acknowledged or appreciated as you would like for it to be at times, serves as a constant reminder that life involves more than just medicine. Your presence alone can motivate your med student to maintain, to the best of his ability, some semblance of a life outside of medicine. At times this life will seem to all but disappear, but your presence alone can be enough, when the stressful times pass, to make him want that life again.

Conclusion

We have reached the end of our journey. I have attempted to cover a great deal in this book, and I hope I have done so in a way that has been useful to you. We first spent time understanding the process of med school and medicine. We explored the logistical reality you can expect during this time. We took this further and looked at the meaning of this logistical reality for the emotional reality of the med student, the significant other, and the relationship as a whole. We explored how this emotional reality develops into a new mechanism for your relationship that I called one-sided emotion work and how it can actually be quite adaptive for a time. We then pieced together the process of moving away from this new mechanism toward a more sustainable dynamic. We looked at a variety of skills, perspectives, and tools to help re-equalize your relationship. We discussed some of the variables present in this process and acknowledged the different ways this process can unfold. We then looked forward and used a new framework to help understand all that is still to come.

Upon my completion of this book, Mike and I have finished med school. He has started his intern year in a surgical residency in New England, and we are much closer to home. We have bought our first house and are also expecting our first child. We still have much to encounter together, both as it pertains to medicine as well as to the rest of our lives. Early on in med school I wondered if we would in fact progress forward together, but after going through the journey outlined in these pages, I can say with great certainty that we will.

In the end, I cannot help but think of the quote by Friedrich Nietzsche, "What does not destroy me makes me stronger." Getting through med school together is hard, but it is not impossible. In making it through med school together, you have overcome an enormous hurdle, and you are very likely coming out a stronger, more cohesive couple than you went into it. Med school may not be the hardest obstacle your relationship ever encounters, but it may very well be. As you continue along your journey through medicine and through life, you can take solace in what you have overcome together and in the strength you have gained together. Med school has not destroyed you; it has made you stronger. This prepares you to handle whatever else comes your way along your journey.

I wish each and every one of you a successful and healthy relationship. I wish you compassion, discovery, and growth. I wish you the outcome you are hoping to attain and the patience, understanding, and teamwork needed to achieve it. I wish you the best along this journey, and may you leave med school stronger and more unified as a couple than when you entered.

Bibliography

Ashford, J. B., LeCroy, C. W., & Lortie, K. L. (2006). *Human Behavior in the Social Environment*, 3rd Edition. Belmont, CA: Thomson Brooks/Cole. 367.

Goldstein, E.G. (1984) *Ego Psychology and Social Work Practice.* New York: The Free Press.

Hochschild, A. R. (2001). Emotion Work, Feelings Rules, and Social Structure. In A. Branaman (Ed.), *Self and Society* (pp. 138-155). Malden, MA: Blackwell Publishers Ltd.

Kübler-Ross, E. (1969) *On Death and Dying: What the dying have to teach doctors, nurses, clergy, and their own families.* New York: Touchstone.

Rotter, J. B. (1954). *Social Learning and Clinical Psychology.* New York: Prentice-Hall.

Vaillant, G.E. (1992) *Ego Mechanisms of Defense: A Guide for Clinicians and Researchers.* Washington DC: American Psychiatric Press Inc.

Acknowledgments

Kim, my cousin, your help has been invaluable. Without even knowing it, you provided me with the motivation to finish this whole project. I knew I needed a sidekick for this last push, and I couldn't have picked a better one. Your editing was spot on, your style helped me remember my own, and your feedback kept me striving to make the book better until the very end. I also really liked having even more to talk about with you on the phone!

Kristen Math, I am so grateful to have crossed paths with you when I did. Your experience as a published spouse of a medical professional (*Surviving Residency: A medical spouse guide to embracing the training years*, Kristen Math) helped me to believe all this was possible. I appreciated having you as a sounding board, and I thank you for your practical feedback and advice. I look forward to maintaining our connection and furthering the word as significant others of medical professionals.

Anne, thank you for your off-handed comment years ago suggesting that I write a book about med school relationships. I think you were at least half joking, but it struck me, and I fell in love with the idea. An intense feeling of motivation developed within me the moment you made this comment, and it never quite disappeared. So for that, I thank you.

Sunita and Tiffany, what would I have ever done without you? Having you both in my life through the med school years without a doubt kept me sane and functioning. You define "empathy-based supports" and the friendship we share goes beyond mere words. In the end, you 'just know', and I love you both for that. Thank you both also for reading my draft so long ago and keeping me honest about what really does happen in our med school relationships. Brian and James, thank you for choosing to marry such phenomenal women, and thank you for allowing your experiences with med school and your relationships to inform the concepts I have developed in this book.

Holly and Jessica... Holly, I greatly appreciate your feedback regarding the mental health concepts in this book and for allowing me to spew about all my ideas as we walked the rail trail. Jessica, you were the best surrogate husband I ever could have asked for. I wish we were closer and you could still fill that role. To you both, you took the notion of "compassion-based supports" to a whole new level; you connected with my reality in a way few were able and you provided me with such amazing friendship along the way. Thank you both for serving as a constant reminder about everything else that is important in my life and for making sure that medicine did not consume me.

Swathi and Alisa, the conversations I have had with you both over the past several years have helped me in so many ways. Listening to your experiences with med school gave me perspective about our own experiences. I often left our conversations with a renewed desire to be kind and supportive in my relationship. You provided me with hope during our most difficult moments by reminding me that underneath all the challenges, you still loved medicine and were determined to make it work within the context of your lives. I found myself listening to what you required in your relationships and striving to achieve that in my own. Your perspectives have also informed portions of this book, and I thank you for sharing those so willingly with me over the years.

Jim! You deserve a special thanks. I'm not quite sure how we permitted this to happen, but you have been indirectly responsible for all the most significant moments in our life: our engagement, the purchasing of our super cool TV, and now the fact that I have become an author. I won't go into any further detail, but I do stand by my dedication of Chapter 7 to you!

Evan, thank you for being such a wonderful brother. I came to count on your yearly trips to visit us, and I loved spending that time with you. You certainly earned the title of 'most frequent flyer'! I cannot even express how happy I am to be so close to you and Erin again.

Mom and Dad, I have too many thank you's to say to you. I of course thank you for reading the book and providing feedback, for your support with the publishing process, and dad, for your help with the cover (see below). But well beyond that, I thank you for being such utterly amazing parents- now, and in the past. Thank you for raising me in such a way that I thought that writing a book was within the realm of my possibility. Thank you for instilling in me the values I have needed to make my relationship work, even through the difficult times. Thank you for your support in our move away; it was hard, but it would have been harder if you had handled it differently. And lastly, thank you for believing us, accepting our reality, allowing us to find a way through it, and respecting the way we have decided to live our life at every step along the way.

An additional thank you to my dad, Don Paradis, and his production team for the development of the cover. Beautiful work, and I appreciate it tremendously!

Lastly, Mike, without you there would be no book. I never would have encountered med school, and I never would have needed to learn about managing a relationship within that context. Much more importantly, though, without you I never would have had our relationship. You are more than I ever could have hoped for in a husband. You have stuck by me and my crazy ideas just as much as I have stuck by you and yours. We are a true team, and I consider myself lucky every day for the life we live together. Thank you for everything, and I love you.

CPSIA information can be obtained at www.ICGtesting.com
Printed in the USA
BVOW070205240512

291001BV00001B/5/P